Wine by Design

Published in Great Britain by Wiley-Academy,
a division of John Wiley & Sons Ltd

Copyright © 2006 John Wiley & Sons Ltd, The Atrium, Southern Gate,
Chichester, West Sussex, PO19 8SQ, England

Telephone (+44) 1243 779777

Email (for orders and customer service enquires): cs-books@wiley.co.uk

Visit our Home Page on www.wiley.co.uk or www.wiley.com

This publication is designed to provide accurate and authoritative
information in regard to the subject matter covered. It is sold on the
understanding that the Publisher is not engaged in rendering professional
services. If professional advice or other expert assistance is required, the
services of a competent professional should be sought.

Other Wiley Editorial Offices

John Wiley & Sons Inc., 111 River Street, Hoboken, NJ 07030, USA

Jossey-Bass, 989 Market Street, San Francisco, CA 94103-1741, USA

Wiley-VCH Verlag GmbH, Boschstr. 12, D-69469 Weinheim, Germany

John Wiley & Sons Australia Ltd, 42 McDougall Street, Milton, Queensland
4064, Australia

John Wiley & Sons (Asia) Pte Ltd, 2 Clementi Loop #02-01, Jin Xing
Distripark, Singapore 129809

John Wiley & Sons Canada Ltd, 22 Worcester Road, Etobicoke, Ontario,
Canada M9W 1L1

ISBN-13 978 0 470 01447 9 (HB)

ISBN-10 0 470 01447 4 (HB)

Layout and Prepress: ARTMEDIA PRESS LTD, London

Printed and bound by Conti Tipocolor, Italy

Wine by Design

Sean Stanwick and Loraine Fowlow   Series Designer **Liz Sephton**

contents

Executive Commissioning Editor: Helen Castle
Development Editor: Mariangela Palazzi-Williams
Design and Editorial Management: Famida Rasheed
Publishing Assistant: Louise Porter

This book is dedicated to my mother, Diane Stanwick, and to the memory of my father, Dr Michael Stanwick. His unconditional generosity and support of my interest in writing were matched only by his fondness for fine wines. I know he would have enjoyed the toast to its success.
S S

For Sara, Dave and Mom, forever.
L F

Photo Credits

Key: t=top, b=below, c= centre, l=left, r=right

Acknowledgements

We would like to acknowledge and thank the following for assistance with this book: Helen Castle for her enthusiastic support for this project from the outset, and always gentle editing; Famida Rasheed for her unwavering and efficient help throughout; Steve Denyer and Jamie Patriquin for invaluable research assistance; Raphael Neurohr for quick and helpful translation work; Jane Holland at Lewis Carroll Communications; Tye and George Farrow of Farrow Partnership Architects (Toronto), for his professional support and enthusiasm; and a huge thanks to Jennifer Flores, for her fluid words on Roshambo and for championing the project coordination effort. Special thanks to Don Triggs, President and CEO of Vincor International for his warm hospitality and generous contributions. Lastly, many thanks to Maggie Toy for getting it all started in the first place.

We would also like to thank all the wineries, architects, designers and photographers from around the world for graciously providing their time, effort, drawings and photographs, without which this book would never have become a reality.

Foreword

The Relationship between Architecture and the Wine Industry

When you are in the wine business, the hospitality element of the business is inextricably linked with the brand, with the profile and image that you are trying to project for your product. It is inconceivable that you would expect to go to a substandard building, for example, if your wine has an iconic intention. Therefore, there is an expectation in the consumer's mind that there will be a compatibility, a parallel imagery between their view of the brand of the wine, what it means to them, and the experience that they have at the winery itself. For example, a wine brand that has a very modern image probably would not fit with an Old-World-style chateau. When we have approached the task of selecting architects for our wineries, we believe that, in simple terms, we consider the idea that wine is about the hedonistic, sensual pleasures of life: the sounds, flavours, colours. So, if you are working very hard to create great enjoyment with the sense of taste in the wine, why would you not give equal consideration to ensuring that the visual enjoyment of the winery is at the same standard? In other words, they are both forms of art: creating a great wine, and creating a wonderful building to house the wine. The consumers, to a certain extent, relate to a brand, both in terms of the design and life style; we wanted to create architectural designs that were very consistent with that.

Don Triggs, President and CEO Vincor International
Interview with the authors, May 2005

Preface

This book has its origins, literally, in a vineyard. While attending the unveiling on the site of the new Frank-Gehry-designed winery in the Ontario countryside, it occurred to us that this combination of great architect with fine wine would make for a wonderful book. There was something so delicious about visually consuming fabulous architecture while actually tasting great wine that we thought others would enjoy this conjunction equally.

Therefore, this book is about architecture and wine, but it is also about the people who make and share their precious product. Wine has long held a close relationship with the buildings that housed its production, but now there is a new relationship developing. Forged by entrepreneurial vintners with an eye both to a new vision of the role wine plays in society and culture, and to the booming growth of wine tourism, these canny business people are reshaping how we experience wineries. Wine and tourism are now becoming inextricably linked as wine clubs, foodie magazines and the wine tour explode in popularity. Many of these vintners are hiring international superstar architects such as Frank Gehry, Rafael Moneo and Santiago Calatrava to design their wineries. Why?

Some of the reasons behind this question are addressed in this book, as are the issues of commerce and art, economics and design. Also discussed is the offspring of this conjunction of wine and tourism: the themed wine destination. Consumers are now able to feed their desire for all things wine far beyond the vineyard, in venues that are increasingly departing from the traditional notions of retail.

Quite simply, wine has never tasted, and looked, so good.

Since the earliest history of winemaking, the physical winery consisted of processing and storage areas, particularly in France, where tradition and provenance have lasted for centuries. In many wineries, this has not changed. What has changed, however, is the expansion of these facilities to include, embrace and actually lure the visitor.

The Wine Tourist

There is a revolution currently under way in the world of wine as both established and new wineries discover the dual marketing advantage of coupling exquisite, brand-name designer architecture with the winery tour. The role of tourism in the wine industry is rapidly growing as both the casual tourist and the organised groups of wine connoisseurs increasingly seek out these new wineries. Tourism is now such a large factor in winery design that the locations for new wineries are often chosen as much for their proximity to other tourist attractions as for the quality of the soil and growing conditions. Inasmuch as the experience of a meal is enhanced by a rare vintage, the contemporary winery is designed as much for the winery tour as for wine production itself. Wineries such as Le Clos Jordanne by Frank Gehry have intentionally factored in the tour as a design consideration. In addition to the design for the wine tour, the dual tourism appeal of a Gehry building within close driving distance of Niagara Falls guarantees that this winery will be a magnet for visitors.

INTRODUCTION

One very physical manifestation of the growth of wine's popularity is seen in the increasing inclusion of wineries on the tourist's itinerary. For example, Ontario, Canada, actively promotes its annual 'summer wine tour' through the Niagara region, with stops at Jackson-Triggs and the future Le Clos Jordanne. Wine clubs are organising tours for their members throughout the winemaking world, taking wine connoisseurship to the level of pilgrimage.

In addition to visiting wineries, the growing numbers of wine tourists have a new form of architecture, devoted to wine, springing up. For example, the Loisium in Austria offers visitors the opportunity to learn about wine while

Right: **Petra.**
Wineries have discovered the dual marketing advantage of coupling name-brand architects, such as Mario Botta, with the winery tour

Opposite: **Petra.**
In the vineyards of Petra, in Italy. Tradition and provenance have lasted for centuries

sampling wine products. A cross between a museum, tasting bar and retail outlet, this new hybrid typology extends the experience of wine beyond the winery itself. Devoted to the appreciation of all things wine, these new facilities are expanding the horizons of how we consume this ancient beverage.

Above: Petra.
The production of wine has always required a close relationship between humans and the environment

Culture and Wine

The production of wine dates back thousands of years and has always required a close relationship between humans and the environment. In *A Short History of Wine*, Rod Phillips states that 'the journey that wine made from the vine to the glass … has always been one in which humans and the environment have collaborated'.[1] As the grape is a product of the land, the qualities of the wine have always been inextricably linked with the earth itself. The notion of 'terroir' in the winemaking industry pairs the characteristics of the land with the specific traits of the wine produced, and now, increasingly, with the architecture.

But the history of wine is also the history of human culture. Whether wine was viewed as a gift from God, or the work of Satan, its consumption has always mirrored the cultural mores of the society that produced it. The role that wine has played in various societies has included religious ritual, daily diet, political symbol, economic driver, medical treatment and many others, all of which directly reflect the cultural and social ideas of their time.

So, what does the consumption of wine tell us about ourselves now?

The Age of Life Style

There is a convergence of influences today that is resulting in an unprecedented interest in life style and quality of life, including an interest in all things wine. The manifestations of these influences include the cocktail culture; the proliferation of lifestyle magazines and television shows; the ease and growth of travel; and the Slow movement. It is the Slow movement that perhaps best illustrates the reasons behind this surge of interest in life style. In his book *In Praise of Slow*, Carl Honore says that 'Fast and Slow do more than just describe a rate of change. They are shorthand for ways of being, or philosophies of life.'[2] In this fast-paced, digital age, there is a growing number who realise a desire for balance in their lives. There is a recognition that quality of life is important, as well as quantity. With this comes the interest in and demand for lifestyle choices. And one of those choices is wine. Wine tours and tasting, both at home and at speciality stores and events, is rapidly becoming a growth trend spawned by a design-conscious, mobile public increasingly focused on life style and environment. Solo Vino in Innsbruck, Austria, is an example of the extension of the dining experience to one of the tasting and sampling of wine selections. Also, the UK Wine Tower is tailored to the culture of mobility and the jet set.

With the growth of interest in new travel destinations and increased accessibility due to competitive air travel costs, the average tourist is now looking beyond the traditional sun and sand package tour. There is a new breed of tourist exploring lifestyle travel. Popular media such as films are also feeding the awareness of possible travel opportunities. The 2005 film *Sideways*, which saw a group of 30-somethings working through relationship issues within the context of wine country in California, has 'uncorked a tourism swell in the Santa Ynez Valley'.[3] Local tour companies are offering customised tours based on locales shown in the film, and visitors are purchasing *Sideways* T-shirts with their bottles of wine. In addition, the film's official website has a link to the Sideways Wine Club, which offers a catalogue of related wines available to order.

Traditional European and North American interests in wine and art are also

Above: Chelsea Flower Show 2005.
Kate Frey designed the Fetzer Wine Garden with inspiration from the Mendocino County area of California

expanding to include a new generation with both the interest and financial wherewithal to embrace wine connoisseurship. Both the number and memberships of wine clubs have grown exponentially in recent years. Hundreds of food and drink publications now exist worldwide, and innumerable websites are devoted to wine information and discussion groups. A further indication of the growth of public interest in wine has been the *Wine Idol* competition launched by the Australian wine company Hardys. In conjunction with the TV channel UK Food, *Wine Idol* is looking for the next TV wine celebrity. Other television shows, such as Jancis Robinson's *Wine Course* in the UK, have both fed and fostered the growing interest in all things wine. Interest in wine and vineyards has even extended into the realm of floral design. At the 2005 Chelsea Flower Show, designer Kate Frey designed the Fetzer Wine Garden. Her inspiration came from the diversified and self-sustaining agricultural system of Fetzer's vineyards in the area surrounding Mendocino County, California.[4]

Right: Chicago Department Store.
There is today an unprecedented interest in life style and quality of life, including an interest in all things wine

The Housing of Wine

Architecture has historically played a background role in winemaking. Buildings were designed and used to house the process of creating wine and, often, the winemakers themselves. Quietly set within the countryside, whether it was Italy or Portugal, wineries simply produced wine. It was the winemaking itself and, of course, the wine that predominated. In recent years, however, these roles have been changing dramatically.

Viticulture has traditionally been an agricultural pursuit, part of the work of a farm or monastery. The process of making wine was undertaken in simple vernacular structures, which were not purpose-built, but were most likely to be sheds, barns and cellars. The first chateau specifically built for winemaking is believed to be the Chateau Haut-Brion at Pessac, completed in 1525. Cultural and economic forces in late 18th-century Bordeaux in France led to the use of the name 'chateau' in the designation of wines, resulting in the first association between winemaking and the buildings related to the estate. This early form of branding was utilised to identify particular wines as products of the aristocracy, as distinct from the mass of simple wine producers. So popular and successful was this strategy that the use of 'chateau' in the naming of wines spread well beyond the Bordeaux region, into the Loire, the Midi and eventually to Australia, Canada and elsewhere. As wine production and public interest grew dramatically in the latter part of the 20th century, so did interest in the buildings that housed the wine.

The public identity of vintners is taking on a higher profile as interest in wine grows and, with it, interest in the buildings themselves. Many contemporary wineries are using new designs by top architects such as Herzog & de Meuron,

Above: **Chiostro Convento, Suvereto, Italy.**
Viticulture has historically had close ties with religious orders

Zaha Hadid and Frank Gehry to stamp their brand on the international market. In the world of winemaking, this marks a shift in attitudes between the Old World and the New. 'Architecture is an arena where a culture's attitudes toward past and future play out in concrete forms.'[5] Vintners understand, now more than ever, that they must invest in the culture of their product and respond not only to the pallete of the senses, but also to our aesthetic palette by promoting the *space of wine*: a place of ambience, of life style, of architecture.

Brand and Identity

The direct association between the making of wine and the buildings that house it goes back to the late 18th century, when winemakers in the Bordeaux region of France began using the word 'chateau' on the labels themselves. The representation of the winery through label design today has progressed beyond merely using the word to using the image itself. Examples of this are the Disznókö winery in Hungary, which proudly displays imagery of the winery complex on the bottles of many of its wines, and the Bodegas Catena Zapata labels that sport a lovely sketch of the Mayan-pyramid-shaped winery.

The significance of branding for the wine industry is increasingly related to the sales of the product. As wine sales move out from speciality retail outlets and into supermarkets in many parts of the world, the ability of the consumer to identify wine choices is challenged. One solution is to improve the readability of the brand. Wine producers who are new to the market are increasingly looking to architecture as a form of branding for their products.

We live in an age of the brand-conscious consumer, whether we're looking at the brand of jeans, car, toaster or even hotel. Stamping a brand is a means of claiming an identity. Consumers choose the brand that most closely matches their own values and ideals, and today the consumer can be a museum or university just as easily as an individual. Public and private institutions and corporations are now utilising the design of their buildings to forge their identities. This is the age of the star architect, who produces a product that represents the ultimate in branding: the signature building. This is not architecture as fashion so much as architecture as identity. It is also architecture as tourism magnet, now known as the 'Bilbao effect' after the tremendous success of the Frank Gehry-designed Guggenheim Museum in Bilbao, Spain.

The Business of Wine

The spread of viticulture to the New World brought traditional methods and values related to wine, but in return the New World is contributing to and challenging these established approaches to winemaking. For centuries wine has been economically important to many regions in the Old World, some of which are still leading wine producers today, including France, Portugal, Spain and Italy. The export of wine is now increasingly important too outside the traditional Old World, for countries such as the United States, Australia, Chile and Canada, as wine consumption rose substantially in the second part of the 20th century. Within the context of continental Europe, Rod Phillips writes: 'To some extent neighbourhood sociability has been replaced by a more intense sentiment of domesticity, manifested by people increasingly entertaining in their homes rather than meeting their friends in public places like cafés … a sea-change has taken place, not only in the amount of wine consumed in some important wine-producing countries, but also in the contexts in which it is consumed.'[6]

Beyond Europe, the consumption of wine has risen, fallen and risen again due to cultural and economic factors. Throughout the late 1980s and the 1990s, medical evidence of the beneficial effects on health of red wine created a spike in the US sales of red wine, which temporarily increased fourfold. The average consumption in the US prior to the Second World War was 2 litres per year, more than 8 litres by the 1980s, and down to about 7 litres a year by the 1990s owing to the fall in demand due to the imposition of federal taxes.

Australia, which has the highest wine consumption per capita in the English-speaking world, saw consumption rise from 17 litres per year in 1980 to 21 litres in 1987, only to decline to 19 litres in the early 1990s. Other countries have also experienced a rise in yearly wine consumption, including Japan and the Netherlands.

China is a market gearing up to explode in the wine industry as well. Fuelled initially by the government's switch in 1987 from grain-based liquor to grape-based wine, the Chinese market is rapidly expanding. The population in China most likely to consume wine as a lifestyle choice is the upwardly mobile youth, a demographic that currently numbers over 300 million. This is more than 10 times the potential market of the US and many more times that of other Western countries.[7] Brand allegiance is strong in China, as shown by the dominance exercised by Coca-Cola in the soft-drink market. The country is still an untapped market for wine producers, but one that is quickly gaining recognition. The potential in China for the wine industry is simply astounding.

In the New World, in the 1980s and 1990s the growth of public interest in the quality of wine affected the scale and number of producers. Many new wineries sprung up in previously untapped geographic regions, for instance in many states in addition to traditional California in the US, in the southern parts of New Zealand, the Okanagan region in western Canada and new areas in Australia such as Margaret River. The stunning new Peregrine winery showcases Australia's national proactive strategy for wine tourism, as developed by the Winemakers' Federation of Australia. In addition to the establishment of new wineries, the scale of wine production is shifting as large corporations, such as Mondavi, purchase established and successful small and medium-sized wineries. For example, Byron in California is a small, independent winery purchased by Mondavi as a vehicle for their experimental growing programmes.

Increased production has been due in part to improved mechanisation, which was previously economically less viable, among small producers. Better pest control throughout wine-growing regions has also enhanced and raised production. Another factor contributing to superior wine production has been improved clonal selection of vines, which has resulted both in vines of higher quality and in pest- and virus-resistant varieties.

A corporate approach to ownership of wineries is now increasingly common in both the New and Old Worlds, as newer companies merge or enter into partnerships with older, established wine producers.[8] An example of this trend is the partnership between Ontario-based Vincor International Inc and Jean-Charles Boisset, Vice-President of Boisset, La Famille des Grands Vins of Nuits-Saint-Georges, France. This consortium has hired Frank Gehry to design Le Clos Jordanne in the Niagara region of eastern Canada.

The changing dynamic in the operation of New World wineries has included a new approach to the business of housing wine and interacting with the public. Not reliant on centuries of tradition and provenance, New World wineries began to design wineries that encourage public interest in the making of wine and, of course, the resulting purchase of wine. Napa Valley in California was on the front wave of this new approach in the latter decades of the 20th century with wineries such as Clos Pegase by Michael Graves. Australia and New Zealand are currently considered to be the hotbeds of wine tourism, with wineries designed by architects such as Donaldson & Warn, Harmer Architecture and Architecture Workshop.

Above: Le Clos Jordanne.
Don Triggs of Vincor and Jean-Charles Boisset of Boisset, La Famille des Grands Vins, toast their partnership and the hiring of Frank Gehry

Countries and regions in the New World are discovering, and tracking, the fact that wine and wine tourism are big business. An Australian study in 2003 determined that 4.9 million international and domestic tourists visited a winery in that year, spending a collective amount of $4.6 billion during their travels in that country. A large section of the official website of the Wine Federation of Australia is devoted to wine tourism. They state that, 'wine tourism has been identified by virtually every state and territory tourism organisation as an important element of the range of experiences being sought by the visitors of today. Tourists are looking for a more participatory style of holiday experience, one that offers them the opportunity to do more than just be a spectator, and high quality winery visitation can offer these sorts of experiences.'

Even small wine-producing areas such as the Missouri River Valley in the US are benefiting from the wine tourism increase: with 52 wineries throughout the state, more than 1.5 million visitors are drawn to the area, spending approximately $26 million in tourism and wine sales. Larger US wine-producing areas such as Sonoma County have now topped $1 billion in tourism spending, placing the industry in the same economic league as retail, health care and high-tech. Even South America is embracing eno-tourism. The Mendoza region of Argentina has seen an increase of 35% between 2003 and 2005, with guided tours offered by enologists hired by Argentine travel agencies. Tourists are treated to demonstration polo matches and tango shows in addition to traditional wine tastings.

New developments are not limited to the New World, however. Architects such as Calatrava, Moneo and Gehry are designing new bodegas in Spain. Characteristic of the new wineries is the access of the visitor to the winemaking process, at least to the less proprietary areas. Winemaking is still closely guarded by vintners, however, and while public access is encouraged it is limited nonetheless. While the traditional winery tour in the Old World may have consisted of a walk in the vineyard, today's visit to a winery in both Old and New Worlds includes the melding of wine and design.

The relationship between wine and architecture is clearly being forged in new directions, with benefits surely to come for both industries.

The case studies in this book are presented in four different chapters. The first chapter, 'Branding the Vine', looks at the growing trend of using brand-name architects to forge an easily recognised identity for wineries including Le Clos Jordanne and Dominus. The second chapter, 'New Vintages', explores the innovative architectural approaches being taken in the traditionally Old World of winemaking that are revitalising the global position of these regions. The third chapter, 'Young Terroir', presents case studies of wineries in the New World that are breaking ground, both in terms of design and in their approach to wine tourism. The final chapter, 'Beyond the Vineyard', takes as its theme the extension of the wine experience outside the winery and into a new hybrid of viticultural design that combines museum with wine-tasting bar.

Notes

1 Rod Phillips, *A Short History of Wine*, London: Penguin Books, 2000, p xv.

2 Carl Honore, *In Praise of Slow*, Toronto: A Knopf, p 14.

3 Kitty Bean Yancey, "'Sideways' Fans Go for Taste of Wine Country". *USA Today*. http://www.usatoday.com

4 http://www.rhs.org.uk/chelsea/2005/exhibitors/show_gardens/fetzer.asp

5 T. Matthews, 'Building Bold'. *Wine Spectator* (electronic journal), 30 June 2003: http://www.winespectator.com

6 Phillips, *A Short History of Wine*, p 311.

7 Dr Stephen Reiss, member first US Wine Delegation to the People's Republic of China.

8 Phillips, *A Short History of Wine* pp 323–04.

Branding the Vine

The design of the winery has taken an enormous leap into the realm of branding through the collaboration of vintner and brand-name architect. The innovative coupling of a recognisable design identity with the winery itself is producing a new breed of winery. Born both of love for the industry and canny awareness of marketing, these wineries are redefining how we experience winemaking.

To define a brand is to claim an identity, and this is precisely what these wineries are striving for, and achieving. In a visual culture, the image of a building is an easy signifier. Embodying both an individual statement and a broader cultural definition, the branded building provides owner and public with a mutual understanding of the product. This is not a superficial exercise; it is not trend. Rather, it is a sophisticated manifestation of the understanding that visual communication transcends all others, particularly today. The global truth of this, of course, is evident in the power of the visual message, communication that goes beyond language; it is truly international.

It is not only the addition of the world-renowned architect to the mix; it is also the recognition of the potential for the winery tour that is breaking ground. Most of the projects in this chapter incorporate the tour as an integral part of

Branding the Vine

the overall design. Interestingly, one of the preeminent examples of this phenomenon is still yet to be built, although the initial wine is already being bottled in preparation for the grand event of opening the winery itself.

Le Clos Jordanne by Pritzker-winning architect Frank Gehry has been designed with the entire journey in mind, beginning with the visitor approaching the site in their car, and culminating with the tasting of the product underneath his undulating, floating roof. Likewise, Petra's design by Swiss architect Mario Botta offers the visitor an identifiable symbol of the winery from a distance, signalling the beginning of the tour experience. Arguably the first by a brand-name architect, Clos Pegase in California designed by Michael Graves, takes the visitor back to ancient Greece and the mythical origins of wine itself. Frank Gehry has also designed the hotel for the Marqués de Riscal winery in Spain, adding enormous tourist potential to this well-established, well-regarded winery.

The exception to the phenomenon of tourism-centred design in this chapter is Dominus in California, designed by another Pritzker-winning architectural firm, Herzog & de Meuron. The design for Dominus has been internationally published, arousing great interest in architectural circles. Perversely, however, this is one winery that was not designed for the tour; it is exclusively private, much to the disdain of the design equivalent of foodies. Most will only ever savour this exceptional design within the pages of a publication. Despite this, however, the winery design has a high recognition factor due entirely to its architectural provenance.

Opposite: **Petra.**
Petra is about experiencing a magical landscape that traces from ancient Greek civilizations to modern Italy. Sporting a mix of futuristic details and old world fermentation techniques, the winery sits in perfect harmony with the Tuscan landscape

Marqués de Riscal

Gehry Partners, LLP

Location: Elciego, Spain
Completion date: 2006

Winery architecture certainly isn't a new phenomenon. What has changed, however, is who wears the crown. In the early 19th century, Bordeaux wineries marketed tradition and provenance. For the last half of the 20th century, the home for innovative winery architecture was in California's Napa Valley. Now, in the early part of the 21st century, Spain holds court.

Located in the northeast of Spain, the hilly Rioja has a long history as the country's best-known wine region and has already seen two distinguished Spanish architects, Santiago Calatrava and Rafael Moneo, design wineries in the area. At the epicentre of this renaissance, however, is the oldest and most esteemed bodega in the region, the Vinos Herederos del Marqués de Riscal. While Spanish wineries are traditionally not open to the public, the vintners know all too well what happens when a star architect drops a signature building on a sleepy Spanish town. Looking to transform its public image away from the traditional Rioja cellar, and cash in on a little of their own 'Bilbao effect', the winery has persuaded Frank Gehry to design a unique addition to the existing 19th-century production house in the form of a hotel, a restaurant, and also a wine-process and elaboration museum.

Only an hour's drive south from Bilbao, their wish might very well come true as the winery's billowing sheets of coloured titanium make the Guggenheim look tame by comparison. Gehry's ebullient structure is an architectural aphrodisiac of colour and form with the fragrant air of flamenco lofting through. If Le Clos Jordanne (Gehry's Canadian winery for Vincor) is dubbed the 'Cathedral of Wine', then Riscal can safely wear the 'City of Wine' crown. Inspired by the elements of the wine bottle, ribbons of pink for the wine, silver for the foil and gold for the wire snake through the winding spaces created by a collection of tightly knit sandstone pavilions set into the hillside. Raised above the narrow streets like fresh laundry billowing in the wind, the canopy creates a covered courtyard with spectacular framed views of the sleepy hillside town of Elciego and the chunky San Andres Church on one side, and the sloping vineyards on the other. When the 3,300-square-metre expansion opens in early 2006, hotel guests will be able to choose from an array of Gehry-designed suites, relax in the health and wellness spa, or even get married in the banquet hall converted from an ancient barrel cellar.

The small 14-room hotel will be operated by Starwood Hotels and Resorts Worldwide and, at a cost of over 65 million euros, Riscal is lightheartedly becoming known as the most expensive hotel in the world by floor space. This is not that far off the mark though. In addition, the hotel will also feature

Above: **Marqués de Riscal.**
Conceptual sketch

Opposite: **Marqués de Riscal.**
With winery design rapidly becoming the new aphrodisiac, it's easy to see how the Guggenheim Museum in Bilbao now looks tame and unadventurous by comparison. With a design that is itself an attraction, the building is lifted above the site on columns, creating a small entry plaza beneath that provides breathtaking views of the vineyards, San Andres Church and the surrounding town beyond

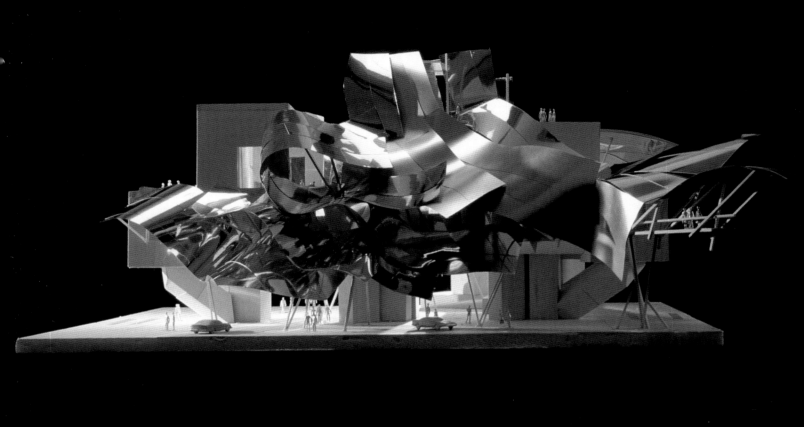

WINERY	MARQUÉS DE RISCAL
ADDRESS	C/ TORREA Nº 1. 01340 ELCIEGO (ALAVA), SPAIN
TELEPHONE	+34 945 60 60 00
WEBSITE	WWW.MARQUISDERISCAL.COM
OPENING HOURS	EXPECTED OPENING IN LATE 2006; CONTACT WINERY
RESTAURANT / CAFÉ	EXPECTED 172-SEAT RESTAURANT IN LATE 2006; CONTACT WINERY
TOURS	CONTACT WINERY. WEBSITE OFFERS A VIRTUAL VISIT THAT GUIDES VISITORS THROUGH CELLARS, FERMENTATION TANKS AND BOTTLING LINES
DESIGN STYLE	A COMPLEX SERIES OF INTERLOCKING BOXES DRAPED IN VIVID AND BILLOWING TITANIUM PANELS
RECOMMENDED WINES & ICEWINES	WHITES OF VERDEJO AND SAUVIGNON BLANC VARIETY INCLUDING: RUEDA VERDEJO, SUPERIOR SAUVIGNON AND RESERVA LIMOUSIN. REDS OF EMPRANILLO, GRACIANO, MAZUELO VARIETY INCLUDING: RESERVA, GRAN RESERVA AND ROSADO
PREMIUM VINTAGES / NEW RELEASES	BARON DE CHIREL RESERVA, MARQUÉS DE RISCAL GRAN RESERVA, RISCAL 1860 TEMPRANILLO AND RUEDA VERDEJO
TASTINGS / SPECIAL EVENTS	CONTACT WINERY
VINTNERS	EMILE PEYNAUD, ENOLOGIST
SPECIAL FEATURES	UPCOMING 14 GUEST BEDROOMS; WINE-TASTING BAR, ELABORATION MUSEUM, LIBRARY AND GIFT SHOP

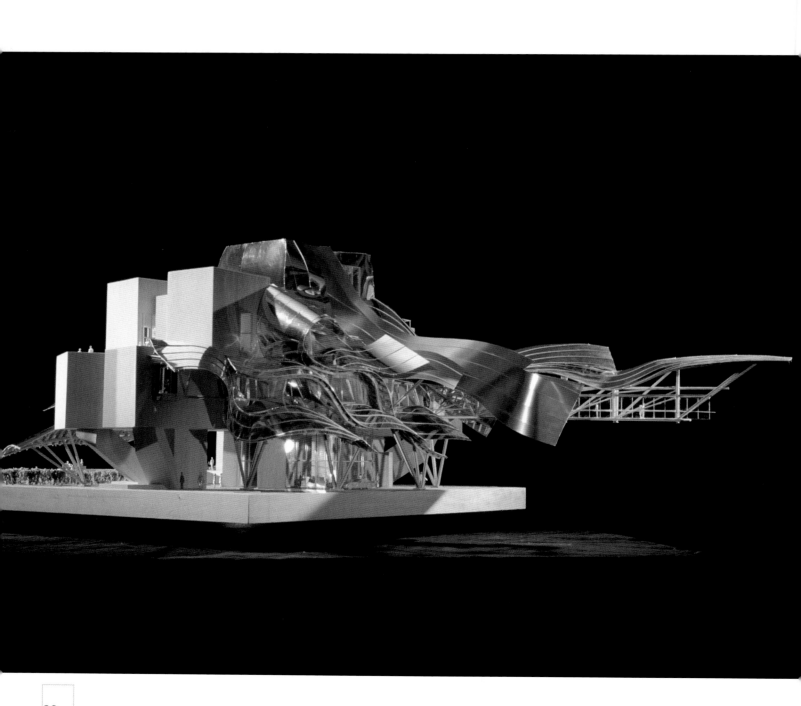

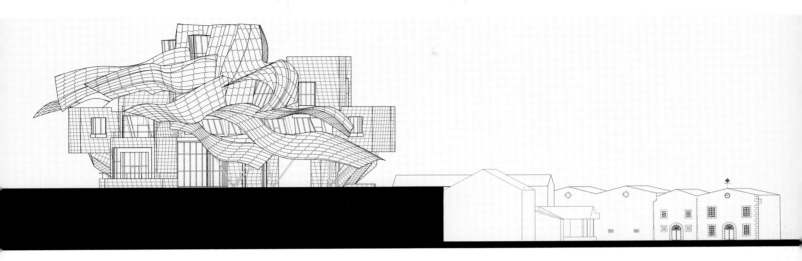

a 172-seat restaurant with private dining rooms, an outdoor terrace and a tasting bar. With the expected hiring of a top Spanish chef, it is hoped that the restaurant will lure tourists away from the Basque region's elite clique of Michelin-starred restaurants.

Drawing attention to itself seems to be the norm for Riscal. It was founded in 1860 by Don Camilo Hurtado de Amézaga, who was later granted the title of Marqués de Riscal. Don Camilo was originally a Spanish journalist who, after cooling off in France from his political stirrings, left his mark on Spanish winemaking by promptly breaking away from the local Tempranillo varieties to introduce Bordeaux vines – of which Cabernet Sauvignon is still planted – French blending techniques and oak ageing. In 1973, Riscal was the first cellar to introduce the *Denominacion de Origen Rueda*, from which it produced its famed whites. Nevertheless, Riscal remains rigorously faithful to its own provenance in the production of its award-winning, quality Spanish wines. Its traditionally elegant Gran Reserva and Baron de Chirel Reserva are consistently produced from low-yielding old vines, while its historic cellar still contains bottles dating to 1862.

That the owners of several wine houses have enlisted the world's top architects to design their bodegas clearly signals Spain's commitment to the future of its wine industry and highlights the depth of resources its vintners are willing to commit to retain the crown. Yet dramatic structures by brand-name architects alone do not necessarily guarantee a fine wine experience. In what marks a decisive effort to embrace the global popularisation of wine tourism and tap into its economic benefits, the new buildings are part of Riscal's 'Project 2000', a growth plan that will see production increase by over 20%. For the time being, however, the winery offers no formal tour but welcomes interested visitors by appointment only and usually with several weeks' notice. While Elciego can be literally translated as 'the blind one', Spain is no stranger to architectural fame and it's obvious that the quaint hillside village sees quite clearly what its future holds.

Above: **Marqués de Riscal.**
A futuristic addition on a grassy plot above the cluster of winery buildings, some of which date from 1860. The vintners sought a landmark that would break free from the image of the traditional Rioja cellar

Opposite: **Marqués de Riscal.**
Marqués de Riscal is one of the oldest wineries in the region. Inspired by the traditional hues of the wine bottle, the roof will be constructed of layered ribbons of red, gold and silver titanium: red for the wine, silver for the foil covering the cork and gold for the wire around the foil

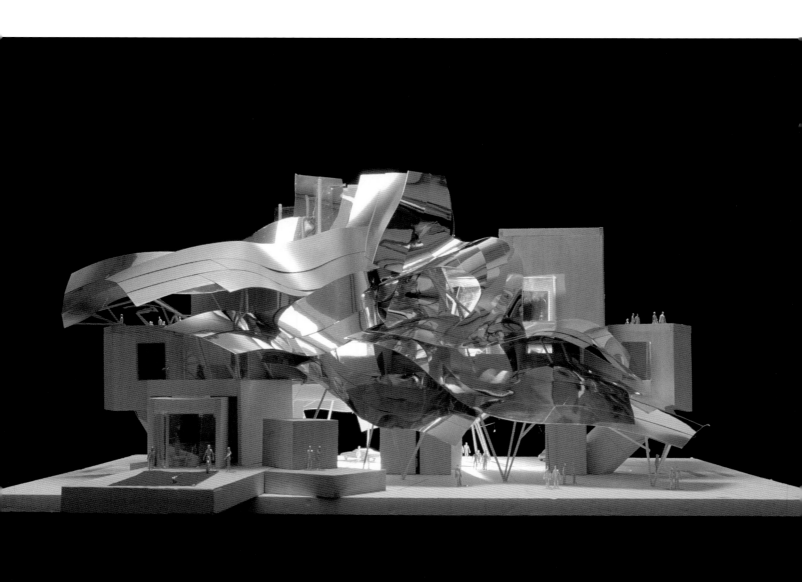

Above: **Marqués de Riscal.**
If Le Clos Jordanne in Canada holds court as the 'Cathedral of Wine', then Marqués de Riscal is certainly the 'City of Wine'. The building is a complex series of interlocking boxes clad in traditional Spanish limestone and draped in vivid titanium fabrics billowing in a stiff breeze

Above: **Marqués de Riscal.**
Echoing the fluid movements of a flamenco dancer's dress, the ebullient structure is a direct reflection of the unbroken landscape and verdant vineyards

Right: **Marqués de Riscal.**
Digitising the model

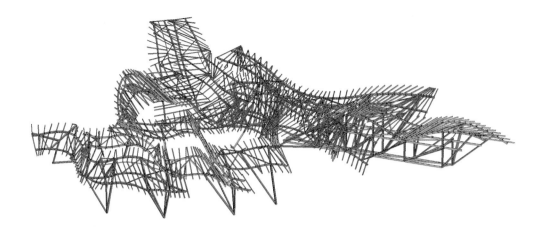

Above: **Marqués de Riscal.**
View of the construction site

Top: **Marqués de Riscal.**
The complex network of structural beams and
purlins seems more akin to windswept grape vines
on rolling hills after the harvest than to the structural
skeleton of a building

Bodegas Ysios

Santiago Calatrava Architects

Location: Laguardia, Spain
Completion date: 2001

Anyone who has travelled to Spain will undoubtedly be familiar with the work of Santiago Calatrava, its foremost living engineer, architect and sculptor. With its wonderful organic sensibility and delicate filigreed structures, it's hard not to be impressed, if not in complete awe of his buildings. What Calatrava is best known for though, is his keen mastery of structural tectonics, whether it be through walls, roof or, most likely the skeleton, and his ability to use them to create absolutely breathtaking sculptural spaces. *Calatrava* is in fact an aristocratic name, passed down from a medieval order of knights, but with buildings that often conjure deep anthropomorphic resemblances, perhaps the story of Jonah and the Whale is more appropriate.

Mythical references aside, the drama of Calatrava's architecture is indeed a perfect vehicle for an innovative winery seeking to spearhead the Spanish Rioja brand in the 21st century. From the start, Ysios was conceived as an icon for the Bodegas & Bebidas Group's prestigious new wine, *La Rioja Alavesa*. While meeting the requirements of a production capacity of 1.5 million bottles a year, (storage and sales), the building would also need to harmonise with the picturesque landscape, a scenic terrain with pronounced grade swells of as much as 10 metres from the lowest southern tip to the highest level in the north. And while vines actually occupy about only half of the roughly rectangular site, the Alava region of Laguardia is one of the world's best and most traditional wine regions, producing grapes.

Ysios is located a stone's throw from Rioja's other star wineries, Vinos Herederos del Marqués de Riscal, currently under construction by Frank Gehry, and the Bodegas Julián Chivite by Rafael Moneo. Nevertheless, the request was to create an inconspicuous icon. This seems to be a contradiction in terms, yet this is exactly what the winery achieves as it beautifully captures the rugged thrusts of the grey Cantabrian crags and echoes the warm gold of Rioja's rolling wheat fields, while at the same time the heaving roof and rolling facade form an autonomous site-specific sculpture. In true Calatrava style, the building is born from a series of undulating wooden fingers of Scandinavian fir that rest on similarly swelling parallel concrete walls. Tracing a sinusoidal path in both plan and elevation, the two meet at the low and narrow points yet burst outward and upwards in melodic rhythm and crescendo at the entry and the fully glazed visitors' centre within. The walls are largely free from penetrations and are clad in a horizontal, light-cedar panelling stained in a washed-copper hue to match the earth tones underneath the vines. Mirrored in a reflecting pool tiled with white,

Opposite: **Bodegas Ysios.**
In the fermentation room, located in the exact spot where the criss-crossing network of wooden beams meets at their lowest point, the highly polished floors and the simplicity of the ordered stainless-steel tanks contrast with the warmth and complexity of the structure just feet above

Below: **Bodegas Ysios.**
Mirrored in a reflecting pool tiled with white, broken ceramics at their feet, the concave walls trace images of a row of wine barrels. A granite footbridge across the pool gives access to the vineyards

Winery	Bodegas Ysios
Address	Camino de la Hoya, 01300 Laguardia, Alava, Spain
Telephone	+34 945 60 06 40
Website	www.bodegasysios.com; www.allieddomecqbodegas.com
Opening hours	Monday to Friday: 11am, 1pm and 4pm; Saturday and Sunday: 11am and 1pm; by appointment only
Restaurant / café	Contact winery
Tours	Monday to Friday 11am, 1pm, 4pm; Saturday, Sunday 11am, 1pm. By appointment only
Design style	The heaving roof and undulating facade roll together in melodic rhythm
Recommended wines & icewines	Ysios Vendimia Selecionada 1999
Premium vintages / new releases	Ysios Reserva 1999
Tastings / special events	Contact winery
Vintners	Diego Pinilla
Special features	Club Ysios – the club for wine lovers: provides the option to purchase one of 300 Ysios casks, featuring personalised wine bottle labels with your or your company's name

Above: **Bodegas Ysios.**
In the ageing room barrels are arranged in an
undulating pattern to echo the cycles of the roof
and walls

to the earthly cataclysm that created the site's rich volcanic ash, the steel hulk appears to have been forged directly from the molten processes afire deep in the earth. But like the wine, the weathered steel has a velvety texture and actually blends in quite nicely with its surroundings. Taking advantage of the slope, the winery will use gravity to move the grapes along their journey, while the caves are dug deep into the hill behind the steel bunker.

Visitors will be able to make a journey of their own. Functioning as a transitional zone between the low-lying grapes and the tall firs behind, the approach will be via a slightly raised pathway parallel to the curve of the hill. Along the way, punched holes in the rusty steel walls will set the view for glimpses of the shiny stainless-steel tanks within – alluding to the science and machinery of winemaking. The monochromatic finish of the steel will amplify the curving bulk of the tasting room, the final destination of the journey and focal point of the winery. Inside, clean-finished and simple materials will create a wonderful contrast to the raw industrial nature of the steel skin. Just below will be the processing spaces, fermentation tanks and access to the ageing caves.

Just as Morphosis helped to usher in a new era of architectural experimentation, and in doing so making Mayne a highly sought-after architect, Azalea is hoping their small but important winery will have a similar effect. Not that it really needs the help though. Azalea is already well positioned in the wine world with its Diamond Mountain Merlot, and its location in Calistoga, about 80 miles north of San Francisco at the top of the Napa Valley, doesn't hurt either. Currently, the cellars produce about 4,000 exclusive cases annually which they distribute throughout the United States. The winery is currently in the design stage with construction expected some time in 2006.

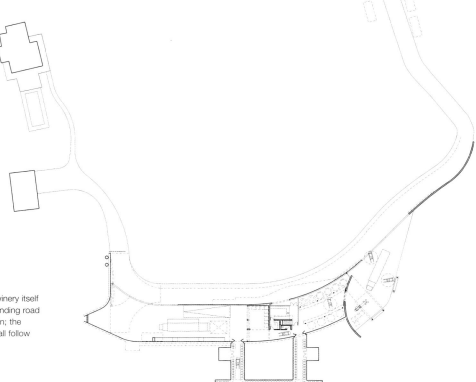

Right: Azalea Springs.
At only 6.5 acres, the vineyard and the winery itself are quite tiny by Napa standards. The winding road meanders along the base of the mountain; the grapes, the visitors and the winery itself all follow this same path

López de Heredia Vina Tondonia

Zaha Hadid Architects

Location: Haro, Spain
Completion date: 2001

Any wine tour to Haro, the undisputed wine capital of Spain, wouldn't be complete without a visit to the López de Heredia Vina Tondonia winery, the third oldest bodega in Rioja and the oldest still under the ownership of the descendants of its founder. For 125 years, three generations of the López de Heredia family have devoted themselves to producing exceptional wines on a par with the best in the world.

When he began to build the bodega, Don Rafael López de Heredia y Landeta probably didn't expect that his winery would one day be recognised as an example to the rest of the wine industry of the perfect combination of buildings and vineyards. And little did he realise that the latest addition would come by way of architect Zaha Hadid, the experimental visionary who in 2004 became the first female laureate of the Pritzker Prize, architecture 's highest award.

The adage that from small beginnings great things may grow applies well to this winery. Over the many years since the bodega was founded, the Heredia family has had a long tradition of adding their built presence to it, and, like a medieval masterpiece, it sits incomplete with buildings built upon buildings in cumulative layers over time. With every consecutive generation of the family taking on the task of completing an aspect of the founder's original vision, this continuing commitment has resulted in a veritable time capsule of additions and renovations that trace the historical lineage. Each successive addition to the bodega has been named: La Bodega Vieja (The Old Cellar), La Bodega Nueva (The New Cellar), La Bisiesta, La Dolorosa, to list a few. Some cannot be literally translated from the ancient Rioja dialect as their origin often lies only in local legend. Walking through the vaulted underground corridors you travel back in time and can sense the founder 's touch in the very stones and fabric of the building.

Like cathedrals of old, work is never-ending and it still continues today. To tackle this generation's addition Zaha Hadid was brought in to design a small pavilion for the visitors. It's not the traditional tasting room one would expect but then again, nothing about Zaha is traditional. Hadid was born in Baghdad in 1950 and trained at the Architectural Association in London. She burst onto the architectural scene in the early 1980s with a series of spectacular graphical experiments and new spatial concepts that intensify urban landscapes in the pursuit of a larger vision that includes not just buildings but also products, interiors and furniture.

Like the skin of an onion, the new pavilion would be just one layer in a larger composition that will keep on growing. The intention of the tasting room

Opposite: **López De Heredia Vina Tondonia.**
Not the usual tasting room, the new pavilion would be just one layer in a larger composition that will keep on growing. The intention was therefore that it would wrap itself around an older and now restored wine pavilion first commissioned by the present owners' great-grandfather for the 1910 World's Fair

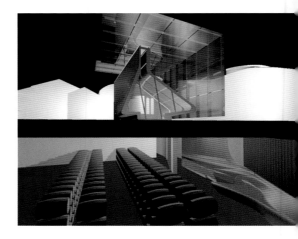

Above: **López De Heredia Vina Tondonia.**
Huge 125-year-old oak casks used for fermentation sit below the new pavilion. These play a pivotal role in the fermentation of the wines as the family uses completely natural and traditional methods of winemaking

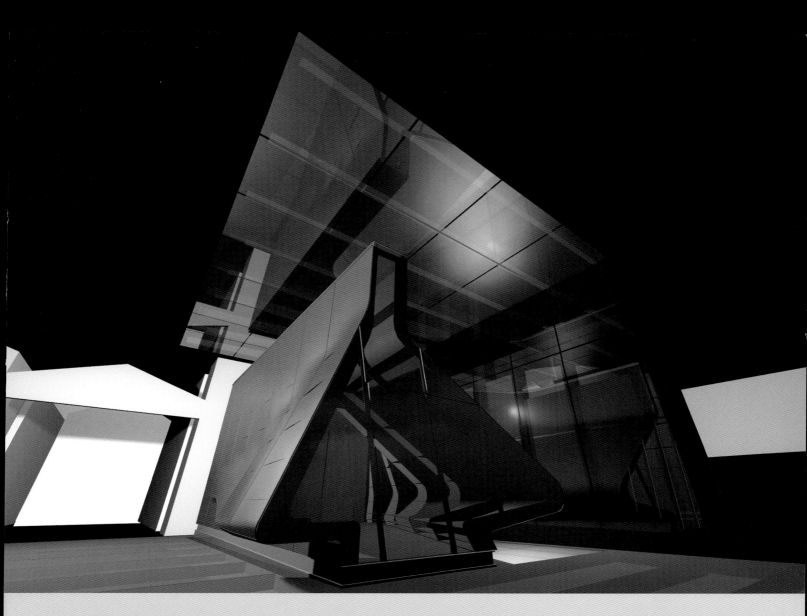

WINERY	López de Heredia Vina Tondonia
ADDRESS	Aptdo No 8, Avda Vizcaya, 3, 26200 Haro, La Rioja, Spain
TELEPHONE	+34 941 31 02 44 General
WEBSITE	www.lopezdeheredia.com
OPENING HOURS	Contact winery
RESTAURANT / CAFÉ	Tasting room and facilities available; contact winery
TOURS	Contact winery
DESIGN STYLE	Like the skin of an onion, the new pavilion is one layer in a larger composition that will keep on growing
RECOMMENDED WINES & ICEWINES	'Tondonia' is famous the world over and its wines have received the 'Diploma de Garantía' (Guaranty Diploma or warranty of excellence) awarded solely to the winery. Special mention must also be made of Tondonia whites
PREMIUM VINTAGES / NEW RELEASES	Contact winery
TASTINGS / SPECIAL EVENTS	Contact winery
VINTNERS	Family López de Heredia, owners and vintners
SPECIAL FEATURES	Restored wine pavilion first commissioned by the current owners' great-grandfather for the 1910 World's Fair

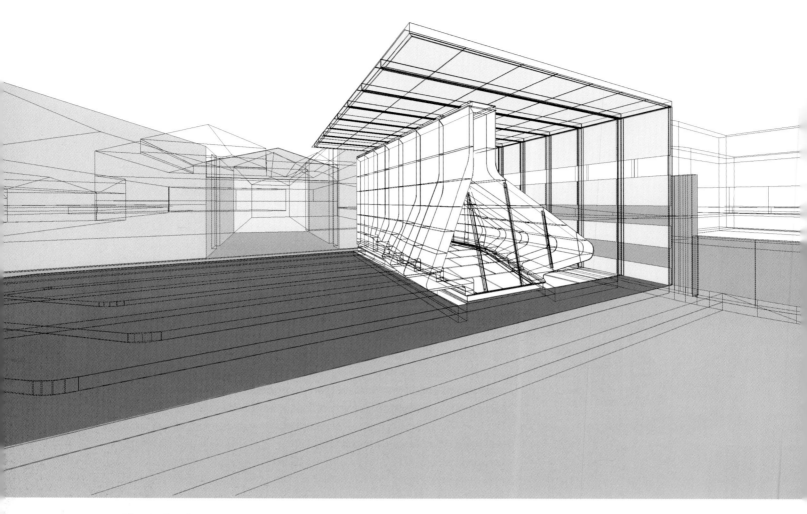

Above: López De Heredia Vina Tondonia.
Wedged between the existing winery buildings, the visitors' tasting centre unravels itself like the skin of an onion. It will become a stepping stone, a bridge between past, present and future developments at the bodega

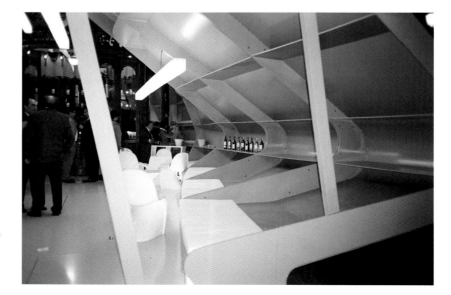

Right: López De Heredia Vina Tondonia.
An ancient jewel within a new steel container. The original wine pavilion was made from well-crafted carpentry and designed in a *fin-de-siècle* style. The new tasting room was first exhibited at the 2001 Alimentaria food industry fair in Barcelona as a vehicle to showcase the López de Heredia wines

was therefore that it would wrap itself around an older and now restored wine pavilion first commissioned by the current generation's great-grandfather for the 1910 World's Fair. In this same spirit, the new tasting room was first exhibited at the 2001 Alimentaria food industry fair in Barcelona as a vehicle to showcase the López de Heredia wines. Afterwards, the mobile unit was relocated to the bodega at Haro, where in time it too will be superseded by a future addition of buildings and extensions. Like the winery it is clipped on to, it will become a stepping stone, a bridge between the past, the present and future developments at the bodega.

Says the architect: 'The starting point was to understand the past but also to look ahead and jump to the future to determine how the present form might evolve.' Knowing the family's propensity for accretive growth, she felt the 1910 pavilion would indeed prove an effective vehicle. As the original structure – which, incidentally, was found abandoned in the outbuildings of the winery – was made from well-crafted carpentry and designed in a *fin-de-siècle* style, the opportunity to let the cycle repeat itself and present this ancient jewel within a new container proved too tempting. Continuing with the onion analogy, studies in form and shape led to a container that grew as a series of sectional cuts. The section starts as a steel-framed rectangle that wraps around the old pavilion and then contorts itself into a 'distorted memory shape' resembling a wine decanter. While this was apparently unintentional, the fact that a new bottle for an old wine had been designed was indeed an exciting surprise. Inside, the polished steel and slick white furniture sit nicely against the coloured bottles and the warmth of the original wood pavilion.

Although this will change, today the estate covers 53,000 square metres with 6,900 square metres of underground cellars which house 15,000 barrels of maturing Bordeaux. This is in addition to the huge 125-year-old oak casks used for fermentation, which sit below the new pavilion.

Above: **López De Heredia Vina Tondonia.**
Computer rendering of the original 1910 pavilion as the steel skin wraps itself around it to form a new visitors' tasting room

Petra

Mario Botta Architect

Location: Suvereto, Italy
Completion date: 2003

When you think of Italy, fine red wines and virgin olive oils probably spring to mind. Perhaps it should come as no surprise then to find a winery that makes both. But if you think the heart of Italian winemaking lies solely in Chianti, then think again. Today, the pulse of the Italian market is best measured along Maremma's Mediterranean coasts, a bucolic cypress-treed region that is rapidly becoming the benchmark for international wine, industry and fashion.

Located in Suvereto in Tuscany, Petra offers a beautiful opportunity to enliven the senses and experience the rich Italian palette of culture, history and of course, wine. Designed by Swiss architect Mario Botta, Petra (meaning 'rock' in Latin) is literally cut from the same stones that were used to construct the medieval wall that still stands around the sleepy Tuscan hamlet. Set along a rolling hillside, the estate spreads over 300 hectares and is rich in vineyards, woods and olive groves, with the shining surfaces of the Tyrrhenian Sea visible in the distance. It is a terrain steeped in a wealth of history and tradition – ancient Greek wine jars still dot the area – and experiencing Petra is about experiencing a magical landscape that traces its history from the civilisations of ancient Greece to the environment of modern-day Tuscany.

To give the winery a particular image, Botta chose to create a powerful symbol within the landscape, rather than build a more conventional industrial complex. Petra, with its clean forms and signature banding, is clearly Botta. On approach the winery sits snugly against rolling hills of vines and, as the land spills past on either side, it presents itself as a dramatic cylinder of brick and local Prun stone, flanked by two *barchesse* – porticoed wings – on either side. Cropped to reveal its sloped elliptical face, the circular crown is bisected by a dramatic staircase and studded with a ring of olive trees and grasses, which change colour with the seasons. Resembling a vibrant flower blooming on the hillside, the design is actually rich in cultural and symbolic references. Historically, the winery is intended to be a modern version of the ancient Tuscan villas where crops were integrated with the layout. Symbolically, it is a powerful vehicle that synthesises the connection between man, the heavens and the earth, as the staircase leads to a raised observation platform where the observer is suspended between sky and soil.

The organisation of the winery is relatively straightforward. Representing the seamless fusion of comfort and functionality, Petra sits perfectly in tune with the Tuscan landscape, embroidered with patterns created by vineyards and the winemaking cycle. Designed to optimise all phases of the production process, the central ring contains the steel fermentation tanks at its centre.

Opposite: **Petra.**
Two porticoed wings penetrate deep into the sloping hillside behind and are home to the *barriques* where the wine is aged in oak barrels. Inside, parallel rows of barrels sit under vaulted ceilings awash with in a dim light, while the earth symbolism is brought underfoot through terracotta tiles of a rich crimson

Above: **Petra.**
Symbolically, the winery is a powerful vehicle that synthesises the connection between man, the heavens and the earth, as the staircase leads to a raised observation platform where the observer is suspended between sky and soil

WINERY	PETRA
ADDRESS	SAN LORENZO, NEAR SUVERETO, TUSCANY, ITALY
	LOCALITÀ SAN LORENZO ALTO 131 – 57028 SUVERETO (LI) ITALIA
TELEPHONE	+39 0565 84 53 08
FAX	+39 0654 84 57 28
WEBSITE	WWW2.PETRAWINE.IT
OPENING HOURS	CONTACT WINERY
TOURS	CONTACT WINERY
DESIGN STYLE	THE SLICED CYLINDER IS UNMISTAKABLY BOTTA WITH ITS CLEAN BRICK FORMS AND SIGNATURE BANDING
RECOMMENDED WINES & ICEWINES	PETRA CURRENTLY PRODUCES AROUND 800,000 BOTTLES OF JUST TWO WINES, VAL DI CORNIA SUVERETO ROSSO AND PETRA IGT TOSCANA
PREMIUM VINTAGES / NEW RELEASES	CONTACT WINERY
TASTINGS / SPECIAL EVENTS	CONTACT WINERY
VINTNERS/PROPRIETORS	VITTORIO MORETTI, FRANCESCA MORETTI, ATTILIO SCIENZA
SPECIAL FEATURES	A RICH ITALIAN PALETTE OF CULTURE, HISTORY AND OF COURSE, FINE RED WINES AND VIRGIN OLIVE OILS, ALL IN ONE PLACE

Above: Petra.

Designed by Swiss architect Mario Botta (the man behind the San Francisco Museum of Modern Art to which Petra bears a striking resemblance), Petra literally means 'rock' in Latin and produces a premium virgin olive oil, which comes from 1,200 olive trees located in San Lorenzo

Below: Petra.

Set along a rolling hillside, the estate spreads over 300 hectares and is rich in vineyards, woods and olive groves, with the shining surfaces of the Tyrrhenian Sea visible in the distance. Historically, the winery is intended to be a modern version of the ancient Tuscan villas where crops were integrated with the layout

The two porticoed wings penetrate deep into the sloping hillside behind and are home to the *barriques* where the wine is aged in oak barrels. Inside, parallel rows of barrels sit under vaulted ceilings awash with a dim light, while the earth symbolism is brought underfoot through terracotta tiles of a rich crimson. Entering on either side of the main rise of stairs, visitors are led deep into the bowels of the hillside where the winery's production processes take place, from pressing grapes to bottling wine. Venturing deeper into the long ageing tunnels, the heart of the earth takes on a more prominent role, dispelling any lingering doubt about the nature and origin of what the casks contain.

The Greeks knew Italy as Enotria, the land of wine, and today it is home to an astounding 2,000 indigenous grape varietals. The brainchild of Dr Vittorio Moretti, Petra currently produces around 800,000 bottles of just two wines – Val di Cornia Suvereto Rosso and Petra IGT Toscana – both of which fall into the 'Super Tuscan' family, meaning they have not been allowed to receive DOCG status (Denominazione di Origine Controllata e Garantita, the highest appellation in Italy) because they have been blended with nontraditional grapes, namely Cabernet Sauvignon and Merlot. The vines are still fairly young, with the majority of the vineyard's Sangiovese grapes having been planted in the early 1990s. An interesting story suggests that the name Sangiovese has its roots in a mispronunciation of the expression Sanguis Jovis (Jupiter's blood). Sangiovese grapes are among the most ancient and valued Italian varieties grown in Tuscany. Petra also produces a premium virgin olive oil, which comes from 1,200 olive trees located in San Lorenzo, still within the Suvereto municipality and part of the Petra property.

Above: **Petra.**
Home to an astounding 2,000 indigenous grape varietals, the majority of the vineyard's Sangiovese grapes were planted in the early 1990s

Above: **Petra.**
On approach, the winery sits snugly against the rolling hills of vines and, as the land spills past on either side, it presents itself as a dramatic cylinder of brick and local Prun stone, flanked by two *barchesse* – porticoed wings – on either side

Below: Petra.
Grapes are received on the second level and distributed to the fermentation tanks below while swaths of light stream through from the stepped wooden ceiling above

Below: Petra.
Petra sits perfectly in tune with the vernacular of the Tuscan landscape, embroidered with patterns created by vineyards, modern stainless-steel technology, and the roots and practices of the winemaking tradition

Below: Petra.
The brainchild of Dr Vittorio Moretti, Petra currently produces around 800,000 bottles of just two wines – Val di Cornia Suvereto Rosso and Petra IGT Toscana – both of which fall into the 'Super Tuscan' family

Bottom: Petra.
Running deep into the bowels of the hillside are the long, ageing tunnels. Here the heart of the earth takes on a more prominent role, dispelling any lingering doubt about the nature and origin of what the casks contain

Le Clos Jordanne

Gehry Partners, LLP

Location: Lincoln, Ontario, Canada
Completion date: 2006

With two Canadian commissions now well under way, *über*-architect Frank Gehry is finally returning to his home country, even if it is via the sleepy hamlet of Lincoln, Ontario. The first project is Le Clos Jordanne winery on the benchlands of Ontario's Niagara Peninsula, a scant 30 kilometres from the tourist Mecca of Niagara Falls.

As with all Gehry commissions, Le Clos Jordanne is the product of a close collaboration between architect and client, in this case a partnership between the old and new guard of winemaking: Don Triggs, CEO of the Ontario-based Vincor International Inc, and Jean-Charles Boisset, Vice-President of Boisset, La Famille des Grands Vins of Nuits-Saint-Georges, France. Together they hope to embark upon a *domaine* for winemaking that will house and realise their vision and result in Gehry's first stand-alone building on Canadian soil.

At the time of writing, the winery is nearing design completion and waits only for the grapes to mature. The site nestles in the heart of a 31-hectare parcel of land on the sloping Jordan Bench, and Triggs recognised its potential to produce ultra-premium Canadian VQA wines, with approximately 75% allotted for Burgundy's classic Chardonnay and the remaining 25% for Pinot Noir. The planting of the first Burgundian-sourced vines took place in the spring of 2000, with anticipation of the first Chardonnay in 2006 and the Pinot Noir in 2007.

Gehry promises that people who have visited other wineries will be in for an inspirational surprise when they enter Le Clos Jordanne. 'We have to compete with Niagara Falls,' he says without expression. Because the winery is small by industry standards, only 3,000 square metres, it was felt that a tour proper would not have the same impact it would have in a larger facility, so here it will be grapes themselves that will take centre stage. By allowing visitors to directly enter the processing floor and become immediately surrounded by workaday activities, the intention is to highlight winemaking as the single event around which the architecture is focused; although this will probably prove to be a tall order.

Set some 500 metres from the nearest road, the building is intentionally hidden from view, and designed to gradually reveal itself as visitors meander through the vineyard. First appearing as a silver veil floating above the vines, the winery is actually a grouping of five individual, white stucco pavilions clustered in a pinwheel, while the free-form stainless-steel roof warps and cleaves to form a dramatic great hall, a snaking concourse lit by skylights above. As one moves closer small pathways, analogous to the space between

Opposite: **Le Clos Jordanne.**
As one moves closer small pathways, which are analogous to the spaces between the vines, are gradually revealed, while the entry is nestled between the cleaves of the billowing roof volumes

Above: **Le Clos Jordanne.**
When Gehry refers to the winery as 'The Cathedral of Wine', this is not simply romantic archispeak. Viewed from above, the winery is actually a grouping of five individual pavilions, each with a metal-clad, free-form curving roof, clustered in a pinwheel around a serpentine concourse

WINERY	LE CLOS JORDANNE
ADDRESS	REGIONAL ROAD 81, LINCOLN, ONTARIO, CANADA
TELEPHONE	VINCOR INTERNATIONAL INC., 1-800-265-9463
WEBSITE	WWW.VINCORINTERNATIONAL.COM
RESTAURANT / CAFÉ	A GLASS-ENCLOSED DINING ROOM WILL BE LOCATED WITHIN THE RED-WINE CELLAR
TOURS	A TOUR ROUTE FOR VISITORS WILL FOLLOW THE WINEMAKING PROCESS THROUGH EACH STAGE, INCLUDING GRAPE RECEIVING, GRAPE CRUSHING AND DE-STEMMING, PRESSING, FERMENTATION AND BARREL AGEING
DESIGN STYLE	A SILVER VEIL FLOATING ABOVE THE VINES, FIVE INDIVIDUAL PAVILIONS ARE CLUSTERED IN A PINWHEEL AROUND A DRAMATIC ATRIUM
RECOMMENDED WINES & ICEWINES	PLANTED TO PRODUCE EXCLUSIVELY CANADIAN VQA WINES, 75% FOR BURGUNDY'S CLASSIC CHARDONNAY; 25% FOR PINOT NOIR
PREMIUM VINTAGES / NEW RELEASES	PLANTING OF THE FIRST BURGUNDIAN VINES TOOK PLACE IN SPRING 2000, WITH ANTICIPATION OF THE FIRST CHARDONNAY IN 2006 AND THE PINOT NOIR IN 2007
VINTNERS	DON AND ELAINE TRIGGS, VINCOR INTERNATIONAL INC; JEAN-CHARLES BOISSET, BOISSET, LA FAMILLE DES GRANDS VINS

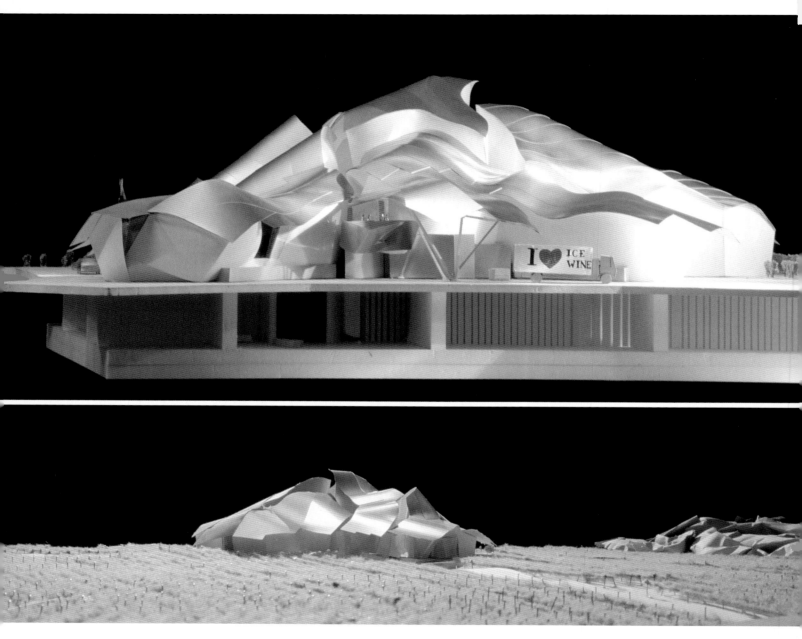

Above: Le Clos Jordanne.
Set some 500 metres from the nearest road, the building is intentionally hidden from view and designed to gradually reveal itself as visitors round the vineyard

Top: Le Clos Jordanne.
A silver veil floating above the vines, the stainless-steel roof warps around itself and the white stucco walls beneath, clearly defining the distinction between the two basic elements: roof and wall

the vines, will become apparent. Once inside, the rolling roof structure will make an immediate reference to the undulating benchlands, while its exposed heavy timber structure will give the impression of being inside an enormous, albeit psychedelic, barrel. Functionally, the winery will operate in a traditional manner over two levels, above and below grade, and will take advantage of the natural flow of gravity to move the product. Interestingly, this will be the second Triggs winery to use the gravity-flow process (the first being the Jackson-Triggs Niagara Estate) and only the third in the Niagara region. Sections for each of the key stages in winemaking, including grape crushing, de-stemming, pressing, and tank and barrel fermentation, will be situated at cellar level and will be viewed from suspended catwalks and pathways above.

By dubbing Le Clos Jordanne 'the Cathedral of Wine', Gehry is not simply giving vent to romantic archispeak. Soaring through all levels in the great hall is a series of glass columns that rise from the underground cellar. The original design for these called for hollow structural glass filled with Pinot Noir, but budgetary considerations have necessitated a change to concrete structural columns wrapped in red titanium, which is then wrapped in glass, giving the same effect as wine-filled columns. Interestingly, glass structures have a provenance that was unknown to Gehry at the time of design. A grid of glass columns and beams was proposed as the main structure in the 'Room of the Paradise' in Giuseppe Terragni's 1938 design for the Danteum, an unrealised architectural translation of Dante's *Divine Comedy*. This unintentional reference to paradise in Le Clos Jordanne's glass columns is fitting, as both client and architect seek to produce a wine-lover's paradise.

While Triggs remains tight-lipped about the project costs, he will admit he has high hopes that the building will speak of his and Boisset's commitment to the wine, and also increase the global presence of the Vincor and Boisset brands. It was, after all, Gehry who recharged our interest in museums with his Guggenheim in Bilbao, Spain. While comparisons are being made with the hyperexposed Guggenheim, the fact that this will be the only freestanding Gehry-designed building in Canada will surely stimulate outrageous tourist traffic not often seen down the quiet country roads of Lincoln. And while Gehry remains deadpan about the potential of his buildings to draw tourists, somewhere between the proven magnetism of Bilbao and the fact that Niagara Falls is within such a short distance, it is likely that at 140 cars, the parking lot is already too small.

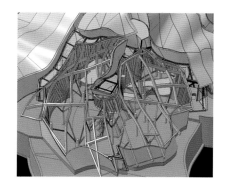

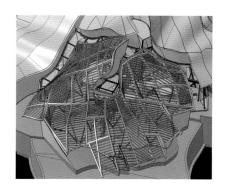

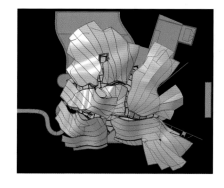

Above: Le Clos Jordanne.
Once inside, there is an immediate sense of reference to the Canadian landscape as the exposed structure will be heavy timber, and will give the impression that one is inside an enormous barrel

Left: Le Clos Jordanne.
Early sketches reveal the vision for the billowing forms that are to become a domaine for winemaking that will result in Gehry's first stand-alone building on Canadian soil

New Vintages

A characteristic of the new approach being taken in the wine industry in the Old World today is the attempt to redefine precisely what it means to make wine in these centuries-old lands. This involves not so much a question of reinvention as a re-envisioning; a reinterpretation of ancient truths that have not been questioned for hundreds of years. One of these truths is the nature of the ageing cellars and who has access to these traditionally dark, damp spaces.

New wineries such as Loimer in Austria are designing the above-ground winery structure to have an intimate relationship with the cellar below. Bodegas Otazu celebrates the cellar with its prominent plinth structure creating an architectural statement that the winery exists both above and below the ground. Although the 'real' cellars are hidden underneath the grassy berms, the architecture is clear about this dual nature of the winery.

A more fundamental development, perhaps, is the changing nature of the relationship that these wineries have with the landscapes that actually produce their wines. In contrast with residential chateaux in the country and the institutional monasteries, wineries such as Bodegas Juan Alcorta in Spain are literally reaching out in the landscape and thereby redefining this relationship.

New Vintages

Likewise, Cantina Rotari (MezzaCorona) sits on a solid base yet thrusts its waving roof towards the sky, simultaneously anchoring and lifting the winery.

An aspect of this relationship is the development of innovative, sustainable agricultural practices that nurture the earth of the vineyard, while taking care to ensure its longevity. Although this may be viewed as traditional, such organic methods are bringing viticulture back to its very origins. Alois Lageder winery in Italy is an organic operation that makes full use of natural energy sources such as solar and wind power, thereby extending the caretaking of the land to the larger environment through green building design.

Another component of the reinterpretation equation is the growing awareness that the external image of the European winery is as important, if not more so, as the internal self-image of the industry. This awareness takes the form of savvy marketing and positioning in the growing wine tourism market. Austria's unofficial ambassador for wine, Leo Hillinger, is at the forefront of this initiative, as his exquisite winery offers much more to the visitor than a tour and a taste. Designed to include space for wine seminars and customised events, Weingut Leo Hillinger offers the visitor an interactive experience with wine and viticulture.

This clever expansion of the traditional understanding of what a winery gives the visitor is part of the larger global development of wineries building the market itself. Catering to the interest in learning more about wine and winemaking, coupled with fabulous architectural design, these vintners are building upon centuries of tradition while taking the industry into (pardon the pun) new terroir.

Opposite: **Cantina Rotari (MezzaCorona).**
Set deep within the 'sala storica', the detailed wooden joinery of the wine racks are home to several thousand bottles of MezzaCorona's finest vintages. Founded in 1904, MezzaCorona is one of Italy's oldest wine consortiums, and its wines exemplify some of the most well respected winemaking traditions in the world

Disznókö

Ekler Architect

Location: Tokaj, Hungary
Completion date: 1995

While it may not have the recognised acclaim of France, Hungary has a long tradition as a wine producer. Grape-growing started in the region early in the 11th century and by the early 14th century wine was quite popular among the nobles and royalty of the day. Today, the most famous Hungarian wines come from Tokaj, a northern region especially rich in wine-growing districts, and offer a colourful palette from light whites through to rich, full-bodied reds. Like many of the former Eastern-bloc countries, it largely supplied the Soviet Union with table wines of rather low quality. Recently though, with increased plantings of standard varietals, the popularity of Hungarian wines is growing and a new market niche buttressed by the naturally sweet dessert wines is opening up.

One of the oldest wineries in the region is Disznókö in Tokaj (the town is also listed as a *UNESCO* World Heritage Site). Interestingly, the Hungarian word 'Disznók 'translates as 'Pig of a Rock', and the winery was so named because of a giant boulder on site that resembled a boar. Architecturally speaking, its lineage can be traced straight back to traditional Hungarian wine cellars, which seem to have slid out from under mounds of earth leaving only their entrances exposed. Disznókö is built using time-proven techniques and indigenous materials such as rich ochre-yellow plaster, heavily fortified stone walls, deeply sunk courtyards, dark-coloured slating and intricate wooden timbering, and it's impossible not to feel its strong sense of history and regionalism, or *terroir* as the French would say.

Designed by architect Deszö Ekler, the winery proper consists of three outwardly radiating wine houses arranged according to the activities of harvesting, processing and fermenting. The connecting thread is a gently curving, wooden concourse which leads visiting tourists along providing them with a chance to view the process of wine production in sequence. The concourse also feeds the sampling rooms and the restaurant. In total contrast to the network of heavy-timber carpentry above, the classical facades of the stuccoed houses randomly pierce the naturally lit space and re-create the feeling of a typical Hungarian village street. But this is not at all about creating an artificial urbanism, and actually has its roots in the traditional cellars of the Tokaj-Hegyalja region, semi-submerged under grassy mounds. At dusk, the mass of the dimly lit concourse literally disappears into the distant hillside leaving exposed a trio of monuments.

Above: **Disznókö.**
Set against the fortified stone wall of the forecourt, the ragwork outer skin of the tractor shed is in total contrast to the warm glow of the skeletal wood trusses inside

Opposite: **Disznókö.**
The slick mechanics of modern winemaking are well accommodated within the traditional wine houses, built from indigenous materials such as rich ochre-coloured plaster and intricate wooden timbering. Here, stainless-steel fermentation tanks work to produce Aszú, Szamorodi and the less well-known Eszencia

Winery	Bodegas Otazu
Address	Road N-232, Echauri, Navarra, Spain
Telephone	+34 948 32 92 00 / 948 32 90 34
Website	www.otazu.com
Opening hours	Contact winery
Tours	Contact winery
Design style	Contemporary concrete vaulting expressed with an historic vocabulary
Varieties	Cabernet Sauvignon, Merlot, Chardonnay
Premium vintages / new releases	Chardonnay 2002, Tempranillo, Crianza 2000, Reserva 1999, Palacio de Otazu Altar 1999
Special features	historic assembly of buildings dating to the Middle Ages

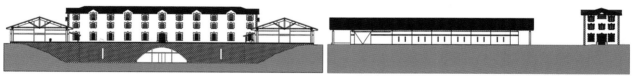

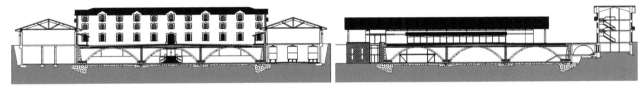

symmetrical bays each measuring 18 metres square, with their massive arched vaults rising 6 metres at their apex. For all its mass, the concrete has a certain subtlety and softness about it. Look closely and you will see a delicate network of imprinted veins left behind from the pine formwork, while the smaller grid formed by expansion joints (to prevent cracking) brings a comfortable scale to the room.

While you don't notice it at first, probably because you are lost in the sheer drama of the space, what makes this room truly unique is that the slender cross-vaults rise directly from the floor; there are no columns or piers providing support. It is a strange effect, one that makes you feel as if you are suspended in midair, somewhere above the floor of a much larger room just below. As the vaults intertwine in constant motion with each other, in a continuous network, uplighting shoots out from behind the oak barrels setting the vaults awash with an eerie dim light that accentuates their elongated form. Beyond the aesthetics, the simple solution is effective in maintaining a constant temperature for ageing; but, more important, it is also reflective of the painstaking care Otazu takes in the making of its wine.

Above and opposite middle: **Bodegas Otazu.**
The two arms of the new winery stand face to face and contain all the mechanics of winemaking – pressing, filtering and fermenting on one side, with bottling and ageing on the opposite side. These three edifices frame a landscaped courtyard; an ideal spot for tasting and enjoying the view

Top: **Bodegas Otazu.**
While the plinth makes for interesting landscape opportunities, like a natural amphitheatre for displaying artwork, the berm actually hides beneath its grasses the underground cellars where 3,000 *borderlesas* (barrels built by the winery on site from French *alliers* and American oak) sit waiting

Opposite bottom: **Bodegas Otazu.**
Otazu is literally built on the foundations of an earlier wine estate. Two parallel arms of the new building flank an existing winery built in the French style in about 1860. Rather than demolishing it, it is celebrated and is today used for the tasting room, wine museum and library

Bodegas Juan Alcorta

Ignacio Quemada Architect

Location: Logroño, Spain
Completion date: 2003

It's one thing to know how good Spanish wine is, but to truly appreciate it you really must know the legend of the Rioja Alavesa region itself. The story has it that in 1635 the capital's mayor banned carriages from passing along the roads near Rioja's cellars for fear that the vibrations would affect the juice and harm the precious contents of the barrels. In a country of wine-lovers, the Rioja is Spain's first true love, and to this day thousands gather every year for La Batalla del Vino, a battle fought only with wine. While the Californians may love their wine, in Spain it is lived.

Rioja is named after the Rio Oja, a tributary of the Ebro River, that flows through the heart of the region. People have been making wine along, its banks for thousands of years. At the epicentre of Rioja is its crown jewel, the Bodegas Juan Alcorta, well known as one of the world's best producers of Crianza, Reserva and Gran Reserva oak-aged wines. Named after its founder, Alcorta is built on what was originally the historic Campo Viejo wine cellars. Located on the old road to Fuenmayor (Logroño), the bodega sits atop a flat plateau planted with vines, and enjoys panoramic views of the Ebro Valley and the Sierra de Cantabria mountains.

The vineyard boasts more than 400 acres of some of the best grape-growing land in the region, and is farmed in individual plots so that the grapes can be selected and cultivated depending on the type of wine sought. Blessed with ideal soils, cool temperatures and a long growing season, the majority of the vines planted are the noble Tempranillo grape, plus Garnacha, Graciano and Mazuelo varietals.

At the highest point of the estate, on La Rad de Santa Cruz, is the winery itself. On what appears to be a level plinth sit a pair of unassuming rectangular buildings, one of which houses the social areas including the visitors' centre and tasting rooms, and the other the entrance to the cellars below. Cast with clean modern lines, each building is clad in a pale limestone skin, with a ziggurat pattern carved deep into its surface. The light skin appears adobe-like and makes the pavilions almost invisible against the bare vines and dry soil. To find the entrance is easy: a massive section of the building's stone wrap appears to pivot itself upwards to become a cantilevered canopy over the door, exposing large panels of glazing set deep within fine crafted wooden frames. Carpentered with the same zigzag patterning, the heavy wooden overhangs extend over the tasting patios to provide shelter from the intense Rioja sun. And as the sun traces its path across the textured skin a wonderful play of light and shadow is created.

Opposite left: Bodegas Juan Alcorta.
With over 150,000 square feet of aging cellars, thousands of oak barrels lie in wait. In a country of wine lovers, the Rioja is Spain's first true love. While the Californians may love their wine, in Spain it is lived

Opposite right: Bodegas Juan Alcorta.
With the history of winemaking running deep within the Rioja culture, it's no surprise that this is a massive winemaking effort; Alcorta is owned by wine giant Allied Domecq World Wines and operated under the thumb of well known winemaker Elena Adell San Pedro

Above: Bodegas Juan Alcorta.
The vineyard boasts more than 400 acres of some of the best grape-growing land in the region and is farmed in individual plots so that the grapes can be selected and cultivated depending on the type of wine sought

WINERY	BODEGAS JUAN ALCORTA
ADDRESS	CAMINO DE LAPUEBLA 50, 26006 LOGROÑO (LA RIOJA)
TELEPHONE	+34 941 27 99 00
WEBSITE	WWW.BODEGASJUANALCORTA.COM / WWW.ALLIEDDOMECQBODEGAS.COM
RESTAURANT / CAFÉ	DINING ROOM, MEETING HALL AND RECEPTION AREA AVAILABLE FOR EVENTS
TOURS	MONDAY TO FRIDAY 11:00AM, 1:00PM, 4:00PM; SATURDAY, SUNDAY 11:00AM, 1:00PM. BY APPOINTMENT ONLY
DESIGN STYLE	A PAIR OF UNASSUMING LIMESTONE BUILDINGS BELIE THE SPATIAL DRAMA WITHIN
RECOMMENDED WINES & ICEWINES	VIÑA ALCORTA CRIANZA IS A MORE MODERN STYLE OF WINE – SMOOTH, WITH BODY AND SWEET TANNINS AND A LONG FINISH; VIÑA ALCORTA RESERVA IS A SMOOTH, MEATY, STRUCTURED RESERVA WINE WHICH HAS BEEN RECOGNISED WITH A SILVER MEDAL IN BRUSSELS AND A 'BRONZE TENDRIL' AWARD
PREMIUM VINTAGES / NEW RELEASES	CONTACT WINERY
TASTINGS / SPECIAL EVENTS	CONTACT WINERY
VINTNERS	ELENA ADELL, VINTNER

Above: Bodegas Juan Alcorta.
Descending the 23 feet into the historic cellars, a pair of opposing concrete stairs ends their intentional straight run at the heart of what is clearly a wine event of epic proportions. French oak barrels piled six courses high run deep into underground chambers, and easily overwhelm even the most experienced wine tourist

Right: Bodegas Juan Alcorta.
In the barrel cellar over 70,000 barrels lie patiently waiting for their day in the sun

Inside, the pavilions are warm and inviting with plenty of light wood on the ceiling, concrete floors polished to a high shine, and long darkened-wood tables arranged in a cafeteria style that makes for opportunities to relax and discuss the wine with your neighbour. At the tasting bar, wines are displayed in wooden cabinetry while the stools are modern stainless.

The two pavilions are interesting in their own right, but they are actually only a small portion of the overall winery as the real magic happens just below the horizon. Set between the rise of two small, planted hills, the plinth where visitors enter the winery is actually formed by the roof of the original cellars below. From this vantage point, the vast Alcorta reveals its true size – over 150,000 square feet of ageing cellars expose their face. Although they are massive, they do a wonderful job of camouflaging themselves – the poured concrete mass with its strong horizontal lines, deep overhangs and heavy shadowing actually mimics the rows of vines growing just feet away. As visitors approach through the dimly lit spaces of the pavilion above, dark earthen colours and indirect lighting cast long scalloped shadows on the polished concrete walls. Descending the 23 feet into the historic cellars, a pair of opposing concrete stairs ends their intentional straight run at the heart of what is clearly a wine event of epic proportions. French oak barrels piled six courses high run deep into underground chambers, and easily overwhelm even the most experienced wine tourist. Currently, over 70,000 barrels lie patiently waiting for their day in the sun.

Perhaps it's no surprise that this is a massive winemaking effort. Alcorta is owned by wine giant Allied Domecq World Wines who also run, among others, Santiago Calatrava's Bodegas Ysios. Designed by noted Spanish architect Ignacio Quemada, and with the grapes under the thumb of well-known winemaker Elena Adell San Pedro, Alcorta won the 'International Best of' prize for architecture at the 2004 Wine Tourism awards held in Bilbao, Spain, and was a finalist in the prestigious Food and Drink Challenges.

Above: **Bodegas Juan Alcorta.**
As visitors approach through the dimly lit spaces of the pavilion above, dark earthen colours and indirect lighting cast long scalloped shadows on the polished concrete walls

Above: Bodegas Juan Alcorta.
From this vantage point, the massive Alcorta reveals its true size. Yet, the cellars do a wonderful job of camouflaging themselves – the poured concrete mass with its strong horizontal lines, deep overhangs and heavy shadowing actually mimics the rows of vines growing just feet away

Above: **Bodegas Juan Alcorta.**
The winery is at the highest point of the estate, on La Rad de Santa Cruz. On what appears to be a level plinth sit a pair of unassuming rectangular buildings, one of which houses the social areas including the visitors' centre and tasting rooms, and the other the entrance to the cellars below

Left: **Bodegas Juan Alcorta.**
Blessed with ideal soils, cool temperatures and a long growing season, the majority of the vines planted are the noble Tempranillo grape, plus Garnacha, Graciano and Mazuelo varietals

Opposite bottom: **Bodegas Juan Alcorta.**
Cast with clean modern lines, each building is clad in a pale limestone skin, with a ziggurat pattern carved deep into its surface. Carpentered with the same zigzag patterning, the heavy wooden overhangs extend over the tasting patios to provide shelter from the intense Rioja sun. And as the sun traces its path across the textured skin, a wonderful play of light and shadow is created

Cantina Rotari (MezzaCorona)

Alberto Cecchetto Architect

Location: Trento, Italy
Completion date: 2004

There's a delightful fizz bubbling over from one of Italy's top wineries, and it's not in the form of sparkling wine. Situated in the Piana Rotaliano, a fertile region rich in vine-covered slopes, wooded hillocks, rocky crags and fortified stone walls, MezzaCorona's Cittadella del Vino, or City of Wine, has opened its doors to interested travellers and passionate wine connoisseurs alike.

Founded in 1904, MezzaCorona is one of Italy's oldest wine consortiums, and its wines exemplify some of the most well-respected winemaking traditions in the world. With over 2,400 hectares extending from Trento to Bolzano (a region that has seen viticulture practised since Roman times), the beauty of the winery lies in its diversity, as traditional vines like Teroldego, Marzemino and Lagrein coexist with new international ones like Pinot Grigio, Chardonnay, Merlot and Cabernet Sauvignon. MezzaCorona currently produces some 5 million bottles per year and has become a leader in the development of the *metodo classico*, or traditional method, of integrated vine management techniques; a practice that has earned the Rotari label a coveted spot in the elite international club of sparkling wines.

Interestingly, the name Rotari comes from the Lombard king, Autari, who in AD 600 became famous for his *Edict of Rotari*, a book of laws that highlights the rules and regulations of winemaking. With these ancient rules lingering in the background, the modern Cittadella del Vino has been developed to spearhead an ambitious vision that will connect MezzaCorona's production and marketing of wine with the increasing interest in wine tourism and wine culture. Designed by Venetian architect Alberto Cecchetto (who also designed the Treviso fashion centre), the winery makes a strong statement by positioning itself as a specialised facility rooted firmly in centuries of tradition yet with a keen eye to the future supported by experimental research and the latest winemaking technologies. It has also been recognised at many architectural exhibitions including the respected Biennale di Venezia.

Like its wines, the winery is an intense bouquet of shapes and, without a doubt, full of flavour. It is a beautiful montage of supple forms that roll softly with the curvaceous hills and then, without warning, thrust upwards in a mass of kinked planes as if propelled from the ground by the sheer forces of the tectonic plates below. The materials are seductive and, although seemingly contradictory, the bulks of reinforced concrete and porphyry stone, planes of titanium and zinc, sinuous laminated wood beams, transparent sheets of glass and galvanised louvres that become porous at night, somehow coexist in a delicate and organic harmony with each other and with the verdant landscape.

Opposite: **Cantina Rotari (MezzaCorona).** MezzaCorona produces over 5 million bottles a year and has become a leader in the development of *metodo classico*

Above: **Cantina Rotari (MezzaCorona).** The name Rotari comes from the Lombard king, Autari, who in AD 600 became famous for his *Edict of Rotari*, a book of laws that highlights the rules and regulations of winemaking. Today, the winery has been developed to spearhead an ambitious vision that will connect MezzaCorona's production and marketing of wine with the increasing interest in wine tourism and wine culture

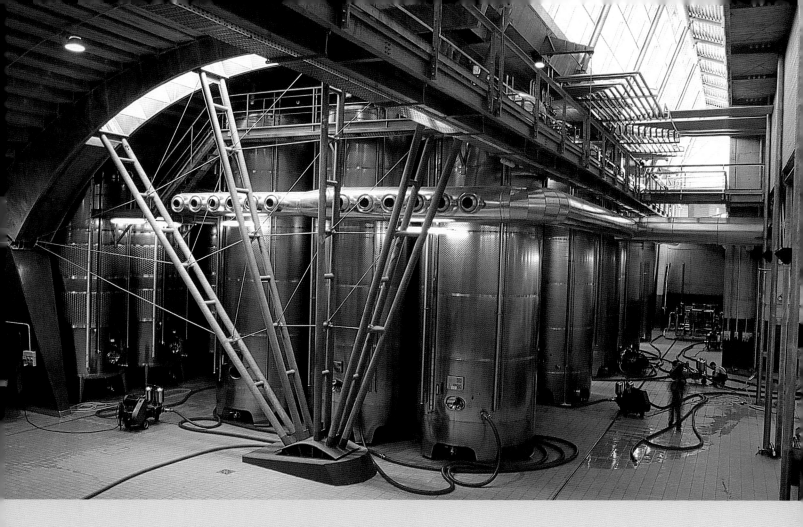

WINERY	CANTINA ROTARI (MEZZACORONA)
ADDRESS	VIA DEL TEROLDEGO 1, MEZZOCORONA (TRENTO), ITALY
TELEPHONE	+39 0461 61 63 00/1
WEBSITE	WWW.MEZZACORONA.IT
OPENING HOURS	MONDAY TO SATURDAY 8:30AM–12:30PM, 2PM–6PM
TOURS	AVAILABLE IN ITALIAN, ENGLISH, GERMAN AND FRENCH FROM MONDAY TO SATURDAY. RESERVATIONS RECOMMENDED
DESIGN STYLE	AN INTENSE BOUQUET OF SHAPES AND, WITHOUT A DOUBT, FULL OF FLAVOUR
RECOMMENDED WINES	SPARKLING WINE PRODUCED IN THE *METODO CLASSICO* OR TRADITIONAL METHOD
PREMIUM VINTAGES / NEW RELEASES	*SELEZIONE MAIOLICHE*: A WIDE VARIETY OF WINES FROM INTERNATIONAL TO LOCAL TRENTINO VARIETALS. *MILLESIMATI*: TWO UNIQUE WINES PRODUCED FROM THE PRESTIGIOUS GRAPES OF TEROLDEGO AND PINOT GRIGIO. *NOVIO VINO NOVELLO*: FIRST WINE OF THE NEW VINTAGE PRODUCED WITH TEROLDEGO AND LAGREIN. GRAPES; *I CLASSICI*: A COMPLETE PORTFOLIO OF SUPERIOR QUALITY WINES
PROPRIETORS	CANTINE MEZZACORONA SOCIETÀ COOPERATIVA AGRICOLA IS THE PARENT COMPANY. FOUNDED IN 1904, IT WAS ONE OF THE FIRST GROWERS' ASSOCIATIONS IN ITALY
SPECIAL FEATURES	'CITTADELLA DEL VINO' FEATURING CANTINA ROTARI FOR THE PRODUCTION OF SPARKLING WINE AND THE CANTINA STORICA, OR HISTORIC CELLAR, THE PERFECT SETTING FOR MEETINGS, RECEPTIONS, BUFFETS AND CANDLELIGHT DINNERS.

Above: Cantina Rotari (MezzaCorona).
Situated in the Piana Rotaliano along the Adige Valley, a fertile region rich in vine-covered slopes, wooded hillocks, rocky crags and fortified stone walls, MezzaCorona's Cittadella del Vino is an intense bouquet of shapes and, without a doubt, full of flavour

In actual fact, MezzaCorona is not a single building but rather an interesting collection of autonomous units, each with a specific function including: the Cantina Rotari for the production of sparkling wine; the Cantina di Vinificazione for processing grapes, connected to which is a large restaurant where local specialties are served; and the Pala Rotari, an auditorium for 1,200 visitors. While each element is expressed differently, this seemingly large industrial complex is best defined by the consistency of its feel and the unmistakable fluidity between the parts. Cantina Rotari sits beneath the massive undulating wooden and zinc roof, which is intended to reproduce the curving motif reminiscent of young vine shoots. Inside, where the precious *barriques* are kept, the attention to detail is maintained as barrels rest on light iron structures to keep them raised off the quartz floor. There is even an experimental vineyard planted on one portion of the roof. At the opposite end, the auditorium, which is also partially below ground, fronts a deep stepped cut in the landscape to form an outdoor amphitheatre for summer performances. Sandwiched between the two is the slick linear administration wing. Shaded from the sun by a low-slung stainless-steel roof with deep eaves of golden wood, the length of glass facade has at its feet a long reflecting pool. By day the roof appears as a solid sheet of metal reflecting the sun's rays, yet by night it mysteriously becomes translucent to expose the activities within. And like a cultivated vine stripped of its fruits, a tilted skeletal galvanised cone rises from the heart of the winery facility reminding us of where it all began.

The tour is equally dynamic as visitors are treated to a panoramic view of the entire production house via a flowing network of raised walkways that snake in and out of each building. Of particular interest is the historic cellar, which hosts gala evenings and special events celebrating the foods and wines typical of Trento, such as the flavoursome risotto alla Teroldego with, of course, the Teroldego Rotaliano as its base.

Below: Cantina Rotari (MezzaCorona). Cantina MezzaCorona represents one of the most renowned winemaking traditions in the world. Every phase of production is controlled and no detail overlooked. Inside the Cantina Rotari, where the precious *barriques* are kept, rows of barrels rest on light iron structures to keep them raised off the quartz floor

Below: **Cantina Rotari (MezzaCorona).** Cantina
Displayed at various architectural exhibitions,
including the Biennale di Venezia, the undulating
laminated wood and metal roof of the Cantina
Rotari reproduces the curving motif reminiscent of
young vine shoots

Below: **Cantina Rotari (MezzaCorona).**
Set within a multiple-height wooden storage trellis,
thousands of bottles of perhaps Rotaliano Riserva,
Teroldego Rotaliano or even the sparkling wine
Cantina Rotari sit quietly ageing in the Cantina di
Vinificazione

Left: Cantina Rotari (MezzaCorona).
Sandwiched between the Cantina Rotari and the auditorium, the slick administration wing is shaded from the bright sun by a low-slung stainless-steel roof with deep eaves of golden wood. The length of glass facade has at its feet a long reflecting pool

Below: Cantina Rotari (MezzaCorona).
Like a cultivated vine stripped of its fruits, a tilted, skeletal, galvanised cone rises at the winery's entrance to remind visitors of where it all began, while the curvaceous roof of the Cantina Rotari beyond frees itself to finally release its undulating energy

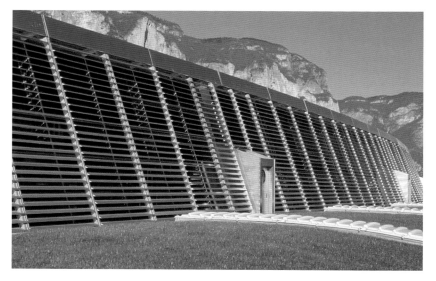

Left: Cantina Rotari (MezzaCorona).
The materials are as seductive as the wine. Vast expanses of glass and a sweeping network of galvanised louvres exist in a delicate and organic harmony with each other and with the verdant landscape

Below: Cantina Rotari (MezzaCorona).
At night the Cittadella del Vino really comes alive. By day the roof of the administration wing appears as a slick stainless-steel sheet, but at night it dissolves to reveal its contents. The network of skylights glows from within the vines

Left and above: Cantina Rotari (MezzaCorona).
At the far end, the auditorium sits partially below ground and fronts a deep stepped cut in the landscape to form an outdoor amphitheatre. Open to the exterior through a 25-metre sliding picture window, the Pala Rotari can be divided into four smaller rooms for performances and specially developed wine-training courses

Weingut Leo Hillinger

Gerda and Andreas Gerner Architects

Location: Lake Neusiedl, Vienna, Austria
Completion date: 2003

To those on the outside, Austrians are particularly known for their beer – a fate often bestowed upon German-speaking nations – while their local wines have remained a treasure trove known to only a select few vinophiles within its borders. But as exports increase Austria's wine market, once dominated by large-volume wine consortiums, is undergoing a dramatic transformation. The pendulum of popular opinion is now swinging to the side of smaller, family-run wineries, much to the delight of Leo Hillinger, Austria's unofficial ambassador for wine.

Leo took over of the family wine business in 1990, and his new winery is a particularly exciting example of the wonderful changes taking place in Austrian winemaking. After years of apprenticing in California, France and many of the world's finest wine-producing regions, he is unapologetic about introducing new techniques and broad reforms to the winemaking process, while still relying heavily on the traditions of his family. Hillinger now manages a total vineyard area of 70 hectares, cultivating 35 himself with the remaining 35 hectares harvested by contract vintners for a total production of about 400,000 litres annually.

In 1997, Hillinger bought about 30 acres of prime vineyards in Rust, an area on the west bank of Lake Neusiedl, just south of Vienna. It is from here, where the soils are of an especially high quality, that his special Hill series is harvested, including Hill 1, a smooth red *cuvée*; Hill 2, a modern white; and Hill 3, a dessert wine of a special class, with an ageing potential of at least 30 years.

Currently, the main focus of production is red Blaufränkisch, Zweigelt, St Laurent and Cabernet Sauvignon, due to the microclimate of the lake and also to the winery's close proximity to Hungary. The enterprise is not exclusively devoted to reds though, and white grapes are of the Welschriesling, Sauvignon Blanc and Chardonnay varieties.

But the real star of this transformation in winemaking is the winery itself. Perched on slender stilts atop the rising bank of the shallow lake, the simple white cube protrudes from its berm, its face of sheer glass providing a fantastic framed view of the grapes below. To get to the wine, however, visitors must first ascend a prominent set of exterior stairs that lead directly to the tasting room. Once inside, the aesthetic is unmistakably Modernist, with highly polished white floors and swaths of green-tinted glass in every direction. Set against the far wall, defined by a set of free-floating white panels that add texture and create storage niches for the wine, the wooden tasting bar cantilevers itself confidently into the room. It is lit to a warm glow

Opposite: **Weingut Leo Hillinger.**
As the barrels age below, a transparent causeway connects the tasting room with the conference and presentation centre at the rear

Above: **Weingut Leo Hillinger.**
The prominent face of the building contains the presentation premises and tasting room, and is meant to be a clearly visible and sensitive mark that appears during the night through a large lighted window

WINERY	WEINGUT LEO HILLINGER
ADDRESS	HILL 1, A-7093, JOIS, AUSTRIA
TELEPHONE	+43 02160/8317
WEBSITE	WWW.LEO-HILLINGER.COM
OPENING HOURS	DAILY 11AM–6PM
RESTAURANT / CAFÉ	MONDAY TO FRIDAY 5PM–11PM (APRIL TO 31 OCTOBER); SATURDAY, SUNDAY AND PUBLIC HOLIDAYS 3PM–11PM CALL FOR RESERVATIONS: +43 0676 333 54 01
TOURS	CALL FOR RESERVATIONS
DESIGN STYLE	A SIMPLE WHITE CUBE PROTRUDES FROM ITS BERM, ITS FACE OF SHEER GLASS PROVIDING A FANTASTIC FRAMED VIEW OF THE GRAPES BELOW
RECOMMENDED WINES & ICEWINES	THE TOP WINES FROM THE HOUSE OF HILLINGER HAVE BEEN BROUGHT TO THE MARKET UNDER THE 'HILL' BRAND NAME. HILL 1, A SMOOTH RED CUVEÉ; HILL 2, A MODERN WHITE; AND HILL 3, A DESSERT WINE OF A SPECIAL CLASS, WITH AN AGEING POTENTIAL OF AT LEAST 30 YEARS
PREMIUM VINTAGES / NEW RELEASES	THE 2003 VINTAGE IS BEING PROCESSED IN THE NEW COMPLEX SO THAT THE ENTIRE WINE COLLECTION CAN BE PRESENTED AT A SINGLE LOCATION
TASTINGS / SPECIAL EVENTS	WINE SEMINARS OFFERED ON A REGULAR BASIS. OTHER EVENT POSSIBILITIES INCLUDE JAZZ BRUNCHES, CLASSICAL CONCERTS, READINGS, CUSTOM-MADE WINE SEMINARS, ONE-DAY WINE SEMINARS, CUSTOM-MADE THEME SEMINARS, ROUND-TABLE EVENTS, BICYCLES AND WINE, WINE-TASTING MENUS; EVENT OPPORTUNITIES ON REQUEST BY PHONE OR EMAIL
VINTNERS/PROPRIETOR	LEO HILLINGER, OWNER AND VINTNER
SPECIAL FEATURES	THE 'HEURIGER' HAS TWO VENUES: THE STEINKELLER FOR AROUND 40 PEOPLE, AND THE KRISTALLKELLER FOR AROUND 60 PEOPLE. THERE ARE ALSO TWO TERRACES, WHICH ACCOMMODATE 40 PEOPLE. THE HILLINGER FAMILY ALWAYS ENDEAVOURS TO MAKE THE VISITOR'S EXPERIENCE UNFORGETTABLE

WINERY	PALANDRI
ADDRESS	MARGARET RIVER WINE REGION, CORNER OF BOUNDARY ROAD AND BUSSELL HIGHWAY, COWARAMUP WA 6284, AUSTRALIA
POSTAL ADDRESS	PO BOX 438 MARGARET RIVER WA 6285 AUSTRALIA
TELEPHONE	+61 8 9755 5711
WEBSITE	WWW.PALANDRI.COM.AU
OPENING HOURS	CELLAR DOOR IS OPEN DAILY 10AM–5PM
RESTAURANT / CAFÉ	THE CAFÉ MENU CHANGES SEASONALLY; OPEN 10AM–4PM DAILY (CLOSED TUESDAY)
TOURS	CONTINUOUS TOURS AND WINE TASTINGS YEAR ROUND
DESIGN STYLE	THE 'FACTORY' AESTHETIC OVERTLY ACKNOWLEDGES THE INDUSTRIAL REALITY AND LARGE-SCALE PROPOSITIONS OF WINE PRODUCTION
RECOMMENDED WINES & ICEWINES	FOUR PREMIUM WESTERN AUSTRALIAN WINES INCLUDING PALANDRI RESERVE, PALANDRI AURORA, BALDIVIS ESTATE
PREMIUM VINTAGES / NEW RELEASES	ULTRA-PREMIUM PALANDRI RESERVE CABERNET SAUVIGNON, BALDIVIS ESTATE CABERNET MERLOT, 2002 PALANDRI SHIRAZ
TASTINGS / SPECIAL EVENTS	AVAILABLE FOR COCKTAIL PARTIES, TASTINGS AND 'EVENTS WITH A DIFFERENCE'
VINTNERS	ROBERT QUENBY, VINEYARD MANAGER
SPECIAL FEATURES	CELLAR DOOR, WINE CAFÉ AND VISITORS' CENTRE

Above: Palandri.
Lively colours and smooth materials express Palandri's playful and family side. The café plays host to over 115,000 visitors a year and was a finalist in the 2001 Gold Plate Awards in the category of 'Restaurant within a Winery'

Right: Palandri.
Palandri's factory aesthetic is reinforced by its low-budget material palette and simple construction

wines, clothing and produce, and there is a computer-games area for children. Certainly no wine snobbery here; the landscaped garden offers live music, a volleyball court and a picnic area large enough for a friendly game of cricket. And not satisfied simply to sell wine, Palandri has solidified the wine experience by marrying its harvest with dedicated tasting plates.

Beyond a skilful marketing campaign, part of Palandri's success must be attributed to the design of the winery itself. With no rolling hills or ancient woods to snuggle against, it relies on its kerb appeal to make its point – that here, wine is a life style. At night, uplighting streams from the big metal and glass shed, floods the cantilevered steel roof hanging above. Functionally, the winery is divided into two halves separated by a large concrete wall; the production side is all about science, whereas the public face is a whimsical mix of colour and art. The prominent roof extends over the hospitality area and provides shelter and shade for the tasting terrace, while its lively colours express Palandri's playful and family side. Avoiding the comfortable familiarity of the picturesque, the 'factory' aesthetic is reinforced by the winery's low-budget materials and simple construction. It's basically a square shed built around a rigid steel grid; however, the steel kinks away from itself to create the sales and display area. The interior is rich in texture and colour. Shooting overhead, the exposed metal beams painted rusty orange and the polished concrete seem to say 'Forget the past and only look ahead', because Western Australia is a young region with a bright future. Frosted panels, sheets of smooth cherrywood and shiny stainless steel, mobile wine displays and bright spotlighting make the space look more like a high-end retail outlet than a winery. So what's so wrong with that? Absolutely nothing if you don't mind challenging the established conventions of wine production and marketing. The plan seems to be working, as the café plays host to over 115,000 visitors a year and was a finalist in the 2001 Gold Plate Awards in the category of 'Restaurant within a Winery'.

Below: Palandri.
Palandri has made a big entry into the wine market with its new production facility and family-friendly visitors' centre. The winery's imposing kerbside appearance is dramatic – and caused a commotion in winemaking circles. At night, uplighting streams from the big metal and glass shed, and floods the cantilevered steel roof hanging above

Evelyn County Estate

Philip Harmer Architects

Location: Kangaroo Ground, Australia
Completion date: 2002

At the gateway to Victoria's famous Yarra Valley and Dandenongs wine-growing regions, and a mere 45-minute drive from Melbourne city centre, sits the Evelyn County Estate Winery in Kangaroo Ground. Born of a growing trend in Australian viticulture that lets the product, and not the tour, speak for itself, the winery represents a new breed, one that eschews the typical process of winemaking as its fundamental *raison d'être* and instead embraces a broader marketing approach for the fruits of its harvest. Proposing that neither the shining machinery of fermentation, nor the dusty oak barrels, nor even the grapes be the heroes, what is actually represented here is a fundamental paradigm shift that no longer sees the vintner's role solely as winemaker, but rather as broadened out to that of entertainment director promoting the theme of wine.

While it is technically a winery, Evelyn County Estate is more akin to a themed visitors' centre and, like most themed events, is a place of detachment. Offering visitors a separation from the realities of the workaday, what is eliminated from the equation here are the pragmatic necessities for physically making wine. With processing and bottling occurring off site, there are no crushing bays, no processing floor, no vats, no oak barrels and, surprisingly, no formal tour as there is technically little to see save the grapes growing on the vines. What is left, however, is a bottle of exquisite Black Paddock vintage, a highly saleable product of a romanticised process, now available without actually having to step into the barrel, so to speak. But this is precisely the point, as the vintners suggest that the popularisation of wine has less to do with the actual process of making than it does with the positioning of wine as a themed cultural phenomenon. Forget boutique architecture and interactive vine tours, this is *auteur* winemaking, with the winery intentionally morphed into a marketing vehicle that makes the products of the winery theme accessible to everyone.

Granted, the separation of 'winemaking' from 'winemarketing' might tarnish the romantic aspirations of anyone seeking an authentic wine-country experience, but a visit here is still a theatrical experience to be sure. From a distance, the tiny pavilion to wine sits handsomely over its charge of vines, and acts as the gateway to the scenic tourist route through the Yarra Valley. And like all pavilions, the drama is in the vistas. Perched at the edge of the vine-bearing slopes, the fall of the continuous bent roof follows the path of the ground and creates a striking presence from the adjacent Eltham–Yarra Glen Road. Visitors enter the single linear volume from the narrow end along an arbour path of

Opposite: **Evelyn County Estate.**
The building is oriented towards the sides of the vineyard so that all public areas focus onto it. As the stainless-steel roof bends to form a wall and meet the highly polished hardwood floor, a punched opening creates a picturesque framed view of the surrounding vineyards beyond; an ideal spot for tasting or just lingering

Above: **Evelyn County Estate.**
The tiny pavilion to wine sits handsomely over its charge of vines. The roof is the signature element and acts as a gateway to the scenic tourist route to the Yarra Valley

WINERY	EVELYN COUNTY ESTATE
ADDRESS	55 ELTHAM-YARRA GLEN ROAD, KANGAROO GROUND, VICTORIA 3097, AUSTRALIA
POSTAL ADDRESS	PO BOX 6, KANGAROO GROUND, VICTORIA 3097, AUSTRALIA
TELEPHONE	+61 3 9437 2155
WEBSITE	WWW.EVELYNCOUNTYESTATE.COM.AU
OPENING HOURS	OPEN DAILY 11AM–4PM
RESTAURANT / CAFÉ	BLACK PADDOCK RESTAURANT; GORDON BROWN (EXECUTIVE CHEF)
DESIGN STYLE	TILT AND SLOPE: A CONTEMPORARY WRAP OF BENDING PLANES, THE WALLS AND ROOF DEFINE THREE MAIN VOLUMES WITHIN AND DRAMATIC VIEWS BEYOND
RECOMMENDED WINES & ICEWINES	ULTRA PREMIUM BLACK PADDOCK RANGE OF WINES FEATURING TWO WHITE SAUVIGNON BLANC AND CHARDONNAY AND FOUR RED PINOT NOIR, MERLOT AND CABERNET SAUVIGNON
PREMIUM VINTAGES / NEW RELEASES	BOTRYTISED CHARDONNAY – AN UNUSUAL DESSERT WINE; 'TIERRA NEGRA' 2003 TEMPRANILLO – CABERNET FRANC/SPANISH RED VARIETY
TASTINGS / SPECIAL EVENTS	EVELYN COUNTY ESTATE WINE CLUB, INDIVIDUAL OR CORPORATE; GRAPE GRAZING WEEKENDS IN FEBRUARY
VINTNERS	ROGER AND ROBYN MALE, OWNERS AND MANAGERS; DAVID LANCE, JAMES LANCE AND ROBYN MALE, WINEMAKERS
SPECIAL FEATURES	THE TONY SMIBERT GALLERY – QUALITY ART IN A CONTEMPORARY SPACE FEATURES IMAGES OF LOCAL LANDSCAPES, JEWELLERY, HANDCRAFTED FURNITURE AND TIN SCULPTURE

Right: Evelyn County Estate.
A gallery features the work of resident artist Tony Smibert, whose work also adorns the estate labels. Sliding perforated metal wall-panels define the gallery and can be repositioned to create a single functional space, whether for wine promotions or entertainment events

show plantings, heightening the anticipation. It is here, at the controlled point of entry, that the drama of the room can at once be fully absorbed.

Visitors can enter one of the four main areas of wine sales, gallery, café or outdoor viewing patio, or simply linger at their leisure. Whichever option is chosen, immediately noticeable are the lengths of custom wooden cabinetry including two wine and food benches and a bar and display case that slide comfortably under the bent roof above to create a dynamic setting for wine tasting, cellar door sales, dining and exhibitions. Move deeper into the volume, and the ground falls away beneath your feet, the distant hillock visible only through a narrow slice in the caravan wall of the tasting bar at the opposite end. Noticeably absent, though, is the expected revealing of the rolling panorama of northerly vines we know are below our feet. But remember, this winery is about the fruits of the fruit. Instead, row upon row of bottles on transparent glass shelves cast an iridescent green glow about the room and indirectly remind us of their source. Knowing that homage must be paid at some point, clerestory windows line the perimeter and are printed with vine-leaf patterns. On the right, a cantilevered timber deck clings to the building and provides an eastern panorama of the planted vines below and beyond. What better way to enjoy some great summer wine!

Never intending to create a signature piece solely to increase sales and brand recognition, the winery also does double duty by providing an art gallery featuring the work of resident artist Tony Smibert, whose work also adorns the estate labels. Sliding wall-panels define the gallery and café and, if need be, can be rearranged to create a single volume for wine promotions or entertainment events. And on Sunday breakfast is served, so this might actually be the perfect place to start a tour of the Yarra wineries.

Its mature winemarketing methodology notwithstanding, Evelyn County Estate is young by grape-growing standards; its evolution spans a period of only 10 years from the driving of the initial post to the production of their vintage Black Paddock Sauvignon Blanc. Nevertheless, their 20 acres of near-perfect north-facing aspect has proven an ideal location for premium grape production, resulting in intense fruit flavours and aromas, and a high natural acidity, characteristic of premium cool-climate wines.

Opposite top and below: **Evelyn County Estate.** Firmly rooted in contemporary winery aesthetics, the fall of the continuous bent roof follows the path of the ground and creates a striking presence from afar

Above: Evelyn County Estate.
The main design strategy was to elevate the floors
away from the slope so that visitors can experience
the entire vineyard from above, while a cantilevered
timber deck clings to the main volume and orients
to the planted hillock beyond

Above and left: Evelyn County Estate.
The winery consists of one linear volume, entered from the narrow end. Custom joinery elements including hardwood floors, and two wine and food benches and a bar and display case that slide loosely under the bent roof, create a dramatic setting for wine tasting, cellar door sales, dining and exhibitions

Above: Evelyn County Estate.
With the roof plane tilted almost parallel to the ground, the building complements the sloping contours and sits comfortably on its site. Entry is at the top of the slope to invite people in and to make a strong gesture to the nearby Eltham–Yarra Glen Road

Right: Evelyn County Estate.
With a view to the vines beyond, even the smallest details are considered and work to tell the same story, as the profile of the bent roof is mimicked in the front door glazing

Above: Evelyn County Estate.
The cantilevered timber deck clings to the building and provides an outdoor patio with an eastern panorama of the planted vines below and beyond. Reflections through the translucent skin mimic the filtering of light through the vines. On Sunday breakfast is served, creating the perfect place to start a tour of the Yarra Valley

Left: Evelyn County Estate.
The design of the restaurant integrates the building with the vineyard. Behind the highly polished red tasting counter, the bottle wall – a wall of rich mahogany cabinetry, semitransparent panels and glass shelves stacked with bottles – casts a filtered green glow reminding visitors of the vines beyond

Peregrine

Architecture Workshop

Location: Queenstown, New Zealand
Completion date: 2003

Wanting to include Peregrine when on a tour of New Zealand wineries is easy. Knowing what to make of it when you arrive is a totally different matter. A cursory glance will easily lead one to conclude that the warped canopy has fallen victim to the harsh winds of the Gibbston Valley. But don't be fooled, for the winery's simplicity belies the powerful experience that awaits within.

Initially, the building appears wonderfully utilitarian – a half-submerged concrete bunker amid a rough landscape, with a contorted tin roof twisting above. Look a little longer and a variety of interpretations begin to take hold. Could this be simply an abandoned hay shed left to the tides of neglect, or perhaps a metaphorical representation of the uprising shields of shist brought forth by sheer geological forces? The answer actually lies in the name itself. The peregrine – or, from local genealogy, the karearea – is a majestic bird that thrives in the rugged mountain regions and rises on the thermal uplifts from the heated valleys below.

While fully expecting the winery to help establish the Peregrine brand, the owners never intended to transform their operation into a themed tourist attraction, although it does offer tours. Nevertheless, you will be hard–pressed to find the expected distractions of retail or food here; this is a winery designed for nothing else save the singular reverence of wine, a place of contemplation, of interpretation and for discussion with experts. Created in response to a recent growth in grape planting and an increasing demand for New Zealand wines, the winery is capable of processing 650 tonnes each season. Located in Queenstown, deep in the South Island, Peregrine sits within the terraced valley of the Kawarau Gorge and beneath the snow-capped mountains of Crown Range to the north. This ideal location affords it a continental climate of hot dry summers and cool nights with the predominantly shist soils adding mineral complexity. The premium production is a unique Pinot Noir, with flavours indigenous to the Otago region. While Peregrine is far too young to have a long-standing tradition of winemaking, the vintners are convinced of their philosophy of minimal intervention for winemaking. And while the winery may be a diamond in the rough, Peregrine is equally proud of the wine diamonds in its whites, made using a combination of oak ageing and tank fermentation. Simply ask owner Greg Hay and he will gladly pronounce: 'The less you do, the more you retain.'

Like the wine, the winery experience shows an intentional elegance and balance that promote the cause at every turn. Visitors leave their transport on the opposite side of the reflecting ponds and take in the terroir as they

Opposite: Peregrine.
Viewed from the contrasting stark whiteness of the tasting bar, the ordered rows of barrels wait patiently behind a scrim of transparent glass. Presenting themselves as a matter-of-fact reminder of the elixir's source, they rest awash with the warming glow, waiting for their turn to yield their offerings, to yield the miracles of the fruit

Above: Peregrine.
There is a certain industrial charm about the foil as it twists to both expose and shelter the partially submerged concrete bunker below. Effortlessly appearing from deep within the shist rock, the ramps descend either to the heart of the operation – the barrel room – or ascend to the viewing platform above. The soaring shape of the wing provides a wonderful frame for the majestic panorama of the Gibbston Valley and the Crown Range beyond

WINERY	PEREGRINE
ADDRESS	PEREGRINE WINES CENTRAL OTAGO LIMITED, KAWARAU GORGE ROAD, RD 1, QUEENSTOWN, NEW ZEALAND
TELEPHONE	+64 3 442 4000 OR 0800 PEREGRINE
WEBSITE	WWW.PEREGRINEWINES.CO.NZ
OPENING HOURS	TASTINGS AND CELLAR DOOR SALES DAILY 10AM–5PM
RESTAURANT / CAFÉ	WENTWORTH ESTATE WOOLSHED
TOURS	DAILY 10AM–5PM
DESIGN STYLE	THE WARPING FOIL THRUSTS ITSELF UPWARDS AS IF ON THE WINGS OF A PEREGRINE
RECOMMENDED WINES & ICEWINES	2004 RASTASBURN RIESLING; 2003 RIESLING; 2003 SADDLEBACK PINOT NOIR; 2003 PINOT NOIR; 1998 SAUVIGNON BLANC (THE MOST AWARDED NEW ZEALAND SAUVIGNON BLANC OF 1998)
PREMIUM VINTAGES / NEW RELEASES	2004 PINOT GRIS; 2002 WENTWORTH PINOT NOIR (WENTWORTH LABEL RESERVED FOR VINTAGES DEEMED EXCEPTIONAL)
TASTINGS / SPECIAL EVENTS	TABLE-SEATED BANQUETS FOR 200+ OR AFTER-DINNER DANCING IN THE HISTORIC 120-YEAR-OLD WENTWORTH ESTATE WOOLSHED
VINTNERS	GREG HAY, OWNER

Top: Peregrine.
The vineyard sits on the terraced floor of the Gibbston Valley, bounded by an existing quarry and the Kawarau Gorge, under the Crown Range to the north. While the heads of shist rock poke from deep below grade, viticulture is now an integral part of this formerly pastoral valley. Hot dry summers and cool nights produce a unique Pinot Noir with flavours indigenous to the region

Middle: Peregrine.
The answer to the architecture lies in the name itself. The warping foil thrusts itself upwards as if on the wings of the peregrine (karearea) falcon, ready to take flight and soar on the warmed draughts that rise from the valley floor below. The translucent canopy actually serves not only to improve the environmental performance of the various winemaking spaces below, but also creates an ephemeral softened presence against the already dramatic landscape

Bottom: Peregrine.
Viewed from across the exterior courtyard, the full monastic character of the barrel room and its distant altar becomes evident. For all its complex interpretations though, the vintners didn't want their winery to be reduced to a tourist attraction. There are no distractions of retail or food; this is a simple place designed with only one thing in mind – the wine

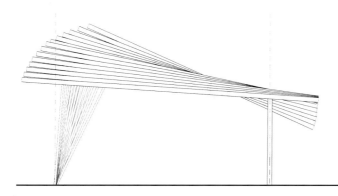

approach on foot, meandering past the historic Wentworth Estate Woolshed – a bare-bones sheep station of shist rock, timber and tin. Entry to the winery proper is via a descending ramp where big sky yields to the forces of compression by the retained earth and rapidly descending foil above. The canopy is actually made of translucent plastic and gives the building a lighter and more ephemeral presence against the rough landscape. But in penetrating the concrete bunker, the transformation – or perhaps reformation – is almost immediate. The barrel room is a low and slender space of polished concrete, heavy beaming and dim light. A monastic air overtakes the senses in what approaches a near-religious experience. Here, four rows of barrels sit in wait as would a patient congregation. Yet for some reason the ageing population remains inaccessible, separated by a full-height wall of frameless glass. While it is not fully understood at first, there is a strange sense of reversal afoot. Then it becomes wonderfully apparent that this is no ordinary cellar; the barrels are in fact the pews and the tasting bar the altar. Sitting atop a raised plinth, the shrine to wine is aglow in a translucent emerald with a sheer stretch of titanium-white marble atop. Against the backlit wall of white, in a spectacular display, of the bottled varietals pronounce their bountiful contents through a rich colorful glow as if drawn from the elixir of those in the congregation waiting their chance to demonstrate their miracles. Handwritten tasting notes inscribed directly on the wall complete the experience; by now, we are all converted. Viewed across this darkened length is a sunken stone courtyard and, further beyond, the softened wood walls of the conference room. After visiting the barrel room, visitors are free to cross the production mass to the sheltered roof terrace and enjoy the breathtaking views of the nearby Kawarau River escarpment. The circuit is completed by descending into the courtyard at the opposite end and returning along a narrow passage against the retained earth and the flinty shist reef.

To be impressed by the winery is easy, and so too is it easy to be impressed by the wine itself. Peregrine's products have consistently scored high in international company: the 1999 Sauvignon Blanc received a silver medal in the 2000 International Wine Challenge in London, and the 2000 Pinot Gris was voted 'best buy' by *Wine Enthusiast* magazine. This is not surprising, as Peregrine has maintained at its root the sustainable processing of grapes with the intention to create quality wines of an international calibre. And whichever architectural metaphor you choose, whether it be indigenous wildlife, or evocative of some cataclysmic geological force, it will bear strong evidence of the commitment made to viticulture by many New Zealand winemakers.

Above: **Peregrine.**
Complementing the philosophy of minimal intervention, the winery effortlessly reveals itself through low-slung volumes and gentle ramps that slowly dissolve into the gravel. The concrete boxes that house the workaday of the winemaking machinery are intentionally submerged in the landscape and shaded by the roof above to control passive climate control in the barrel room

Top: **Peregrine.**
Roof geometry

Above: Peregrine.

The winery displays an intentional elegance and balance that promote the wine cause at every turn. Speaking a similar language to the barrel room, the tasting bar is a wonderfully utilitarian object in its space, not unlike the barrels themselves. Awash with an emerald glow, the coloured mass brings a splash of brightness to an otherwise cold space

Right: Peregrine.

Cross section

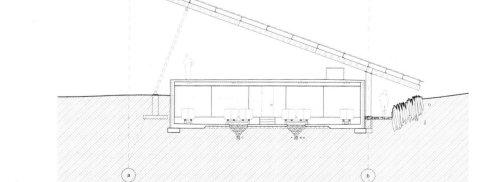

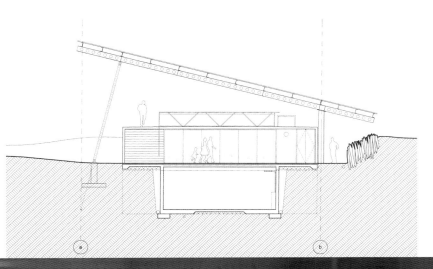

Left: **Peregrine.**

Cross section

Below: **Peregrine.**

In a ghost-like reflection of itself, the tasting bar seems to exude a wonderful ephemeral turquoise glow in the glass. Looking across the waiting congregation of barrels, the wooden walls of the conference room beyond provide a comforting space ideal for contemplation, and discussion with experts

Opposite: Peregrine.
Waiting patiently, the congregation aligns in ordered rows to pay homage to the raised altar that is the tasting bar. Aglow in a translucent emerald and set against the backlit display case, an equally ordered display of bottled varietals announces their bountiful contents through a rich colourful glow

Left: Peregrine.
It becomes apparent very soon that this is no ordinary wine cellar. The barrel room is a low and slender space of polished concrete, heavy beaming and dim light – a space that approaches the religious. Sitting atop a raised plinth, the altar that is the tasting bar is aglow in a translucent turquoise with a contrasting stretch of sleek titanium-white marble atop

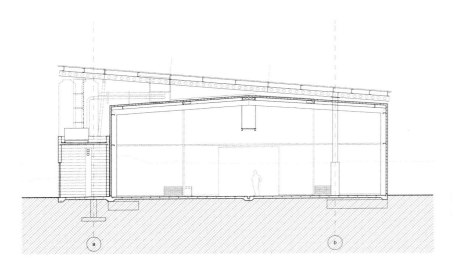

Left: Peregrine.

Cross section

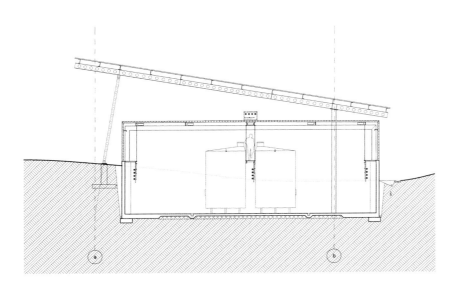

Left: Peregrine.

Cross section

Jackson-Triggs Niagara Estate

Kuwabara Payne McKenna Blumberg Architects (KPMB)

Location: Niagara-on-the-Lake, Ontario, Canada
Completion date: 2001

Ask any vintner about terroir and they will gleefully illuminate how each and every grape is completely influenced by the soil from which it grows. Ask architects Kuwabara Payne McKenna Blumberg (KPMB) about the Jackson-Triggs Niagara Estate winery and you will probably get a similar answer. In a place where wine is the hero, it is no accident that production, architecture and tour are cut from the same vine and bottled into a finely tuned, experience.

At the helm of the operation is the enigmatic Don Triggs, CEO of the Ontario-based Vincor International Inc, and the client for whom Frank Gehry designed his first freestanding building in Canada: Le Clos Jordanne. Vincor is North America's fourth largest producer and marketer of wines, and wanted a building that would support the growth and international reputation of Canadian-made products while simultaneously enhancing the agro-tourist experience for vinophiles embarking on the Niagara Wine Tour – an annual Ontario summer ritual.

Interestingly, for all their combined experience neither Triggs nor KPMB had ever designed a new winery before. Several trips through the Napa Valley proved invaluable as the team learnt at first-hand the techniques of the gravity-flow process. But more importantly, the Napa trips made clear the benefits of marrying the science of winemaking with the art of winemarketing.

If it is indeed true that soil, climate and orientation impart unique qualities to each individual grape, then the same can easily be said of the building itself. Sited to maximise the arable vineyard area and to benefit from the dense greenery on the Two Mile Creek edge, the winery is typically KPMB who, like a good Merlot, rely on a refined and subtle blend of local ingredients. Far removed from the typical European chateau, it has more in common with its rural ancestors. Seeing it set upon a plinth of natural stone, with exposed beams of fir, spears of aluminium and random shafts of light, one cannot help but feel as if one has stumbled upon a country barn long forgotten.

Operating more like a carefully choreographed theatrical event, the tour is a wonderfully fluid experience that physically mimics the gravity-flow process itself. It is hosted by the same person from start to finish and visitors literally flow along with the wine and follow the sequence from vine and fruit to bottling and sales, with of course stops for tasting and reflection along the way. Although it's not formally part of the tour proper, the opening act begins in the meandering approach through several small vineyards. The official tour starts in the great hall, a mammoth cut through the whole of the building with enormous barn-like sliding doors that allow the winery to open itself freely to

Above: **Jackson-Triggs Niagara Estate.**
Overlooking the vines, the winery with its great hall is a sensitive progeny of a strong Canadian regionalism with every detail inspired by the traditional farm buildings of the area

Opposite: **Jackson-Triggs Niagara Estate.**
Visitors descend into the underground barrel cellar which features a concrete vaulted ceiling and an integrated entertainment zone for special tastings and dinners. The heat-sink effect of the surrounding earth maintains a stable, cool and humid environment ideal for barrel-ageing

WINERY	JACKSON-TRIGGS NIAGARA ESTATE
ADDRESS	2145 NIAGARA STONE ROAD (REGIONAL ROAD 55), NIAGARA-ON-THE-LAKE, ONTARIO, CANADA
TELEPHONE	+1 866 589 4637
WEBSITE	WWW.JACKSONTRIGGSWINERY.COM
OPENING HOURS	MAY TO OCTOBER: DAILY 10.30 AM–6.30PM; NOVEMBER TO APRIL SUNDAY–FRIDAY 10:30AM–5:30PM, SATURDAY 10:30AM–6:30PM (CLOSED CHRISTMAS DAY, EASTER SUNDAY)
TOURS	MAY TO OCTOBER EVERY HALF-HOUR 10:30AM–5:30PM; NOVEMBER TO APRIL MONDAY–FRIDAY, EVERY HOUR 10:30AM–4:30PM; SATURDAY, SUNDAY EVERY HALF-HOUR 10:30AM–5:30PM; SPECIAL AFTER-HOURS TOURS ALSO AVAILABLE
DESIGN STYLE	A STRONG CANADIAN REGIONALISM INSPIRED BY THE TRADITIONAL AGRARIAN FARM BUILDINGS OF THE AREA
RECOMMENDED WINES & ICEWINES	SUPER AND ULTRA PREMIUM VQA WINES INCLUDING: 2002 CHARDONNAY (DELAINE VINEYARD); 2002 LATE HARVEST VIDAL (PROPRIETORS' RESERVE); 2002 RIESLING ICEWINE (PROPRIETORS' GRAND RESERVE)
PREMIUM VINTAGES / NEW RELEASES	2002 CABERNET-MERLOT (DV); 2001 METHODE CLASSIQUE (PGR); 2002 CABERNET FRANC ICEWINE (PGR)
TASTINGS / SPECIAL EVENTS	TWILIGHT IN THE VINEYARD: LIVE PERFORMANCES; SAVOUR THE SIGHTS / EXPLORE YOUR SENSES DINNER: A UNIQUE 'SELF DISCOVERY' TOUR OF WINE AND FOOD
VINTNERS	TOM SEAVER, WINEMAKER; KRISTINE CASEY, ASSISTANT WINEMAKER; TERRY MCLEARY, DIRECTOR OF VINEYARD OPERATIONS

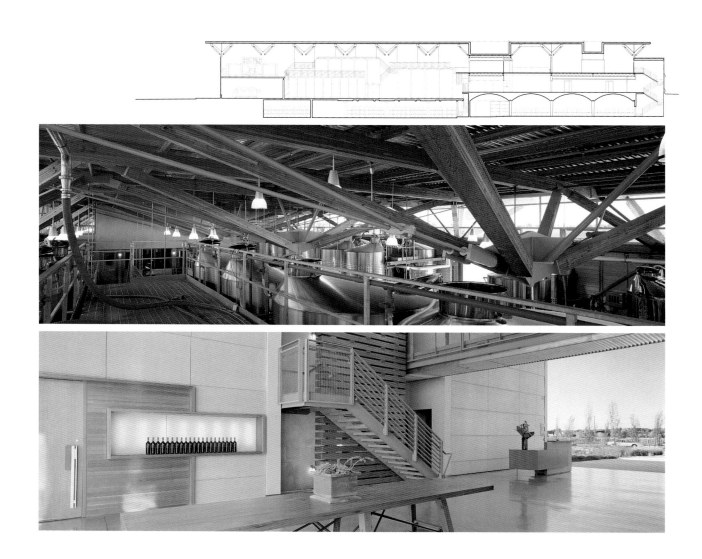

the panorama and the seasonal summer breezes blowing from the vineyards beyond. Here, sliding oak screens echo the winery's agrarian roots and speak to the barrels lying in wait in the cellars below, while polished white marble tasting counters provide a neutral backdrop for the vibrant colours of the wines displayed in recessed wall niches. Once greeted, visitors ascend an exterior ramp to penetrate the space of the wooden rafters of the fermentation room, where a series of suspended catwalks provides aerial viewing of the crushing vats and stainless-steel fermentation tanks below. From here visitors pass, and wedge precariously between the massive tanks and descend directly to the cellar, a dimly lit concrete barrel-vault, and its oak charges. But as expected, the wine takes centre stage and for all the modern cadence and polished tones, time stands still in the warm presence of the rows of ageing barrels.

From the silence of the cellar, visitors reascend to the tasting gallery and in the final act, are treated to a variety of wines, a brief lesson on appropriate glass selection and, hopefully, a lasting appreciation of viticulture and the winemaking environment. As an encore, the winery also supports intensive hospitality dinner events ranging from VIP tastings for two to special events in an entertainment zone in the cellar, eight-course dinners for 100 guests and, recently, live performances in an outdoor amphitheatre.

Through the new winery, sales, production and brand perception have all enjoyed tremendous growth and, most importantly, Jackson-Triggs has been able to maximise its guest service and has become the destination of choice for wine-lovers, tourists and architecture aficionados. Named 'Best Canadian Winery' at Vinitaly 2002 in Verona, the portfolio currently consists of VQA table wines, sparkling and icewines, carrying either the black Proprietors' Reserve label, or the more rare, gold Grand Reserve, reserved for limited edition wines available exclusively at the winery.

Opposite from above:

Jackson-Triggs Niagara Estate.
Longitudinal section

Jackson-Triggs Niagara Estate.
The fermentation cellar features 60-foot clear-span, inverted Douglas fir trusses which extend through the clerestory glazing to support the roof overhang, while a network of catwalks provides platforms for viewing the winemaking process

Jackson-Triggs Niagara Estate.
Wood panelling and sliding oak screens refer to the barrels lying in wait in the cellars, while polished white marble and solid wood tasting counters provide a neutral backdrop for the vibrant colours of the wines

Jackson-Triggs Niagara Estate.
At the main entrance, the double-height great hall becomes a fully convertible space as the enormous barn-like sliding doors allow the winery to open itself freely to the seasonal breezes blowing from the vineyards

Below: **Jackson-Triggs Niagara Estate.**
Cross section showing the great hall

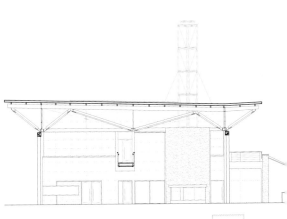

Right: Jackson-Triggs Niagara Estate.
The winery provides a romantic backdrop for
evening performances in the amphitheatre set
among the vines

Below: **Jackson-Triggs Niagara Estate.**
Born of the desire to merge contemporary winemaking technologies with an authentic architectural response, the simple massing marries the process of wine production, the wine tour and administrative functions under a single continuous floating roof

Above: **Jackson-Triggs Niagara Estate.**
The gravity-flow system was adapted as a metaphor for the choreography of the winery tour. In the final act, visitors reascend to the tasting gallery and retail shop to appreciate the product at first-hand

Right: **Jackson-Triggs Niagara Estate.**
Site plan

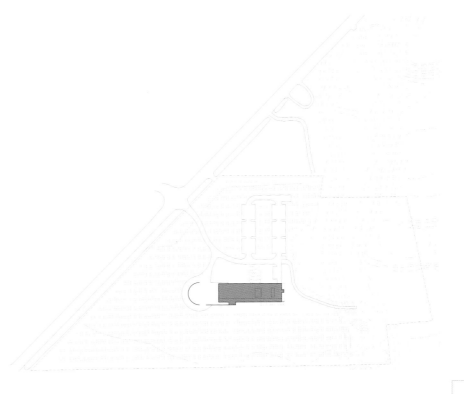

Bodegas Pérez Cruz

José Cruz Ovalle Architects

Location: Maipo Valley, Chile
Completion date: 2001

The most recent news from wine circles is that Chile is shedding its skin as a country with a limited repertoire of wines, and is experiencing a dramatic metamorphosis as it earns a new reputation as an up-and-coming wine producer. Chilean wines are enjoying an increase in international popularity and their wineries are readying themselves for the expected migrations of wine tourists.

An enhanced focus on the quality of its vines, the development of new growing regions and an increased diversity in varietals are largely the reason for the change, but a key factor remains a simple desire to produce better quality wines. One of the more popular wineries is the family-run Bodegas Pérez Cruz. Carved out of the family's 526-hectare farm in the Maipo Valley, 45 kilometres southeast of Santiago, the 530-hectare vineyard dedicated largely to Cabernet reds sits in the foothills of the Andes and enjoys a temperate, almost Mediterranean, climate perfect for wine-growing.

When the Pérez Cruz family decided to expand its wine operations, they held a local design competition which was won by José Cruz Ovalle, thanks to his unique understanding of the particularities of the Chilean land and culture. Yet for all the potential marketing advantages of catering to the increasingly chic wine tourist, Pérez Cruz is a winery plain and simple, and the family intentionally chose to leave behind all the extraneous add-ons like a restaurant or hotel. But just because a building has the utilitarian function of de-stemming or grape pressing, it doesn't mean it has to abandon all the creative potential that architecture and culture can offer.

Ovalle's simple wooden shed springs from the soil through a sinuous network of arched ribs that organically express the activities within, while at the same time referring to Chile's rural periphery. Set on a base of rough-set stones, the winery appears at first glance to be a straightforward box wrapped in a delicate filigree of fruitless vines that cling to the building. Made of laminated wood from sustainable sources, it is beautifully elegant with minimal adornments, giving visitors the chance to marvel at the purity of the forms and structure. Scratch the surface though, and Cruz's affinity for the dramatic unveils itself.

The winery is in fact a series of perfectly proportioned, parallel barrel-vaults connected by a continuous disjointed roof, which bends and curves as it drapes over the enormous vaults below. Recalling the traditions of winemaking, these house great stainless-steel fermenting tanks, oak barrels and glass bottles for ageing, and also smaller secondary rooms for research

Above: **Bodegas Pérez Cruz.**
Against the setting sun, sinuous wooden vines and deep eaves cast seductive shadows on the curved walls of the vaults, while the wood glows a warm red

Opposite: **Bodegas Pérez Cruz.**
As the concrete piers and heavy roof break free from their walls, the roof appears to float, awash with dim light from above and from recessed lights in the polished concrete floor

WINERY	BODEGAS PÉREZ CRUZ
ADDRESS	ESTADO 337 OF 825, SANTIAGO, CHILE
TELEPHONE	+56 2 639 9622/ 2 824 2405
WEBSITE	WWW.PEREZCRUZ.COM
OPENING HOURS	CONTACT WINERY
TOURS	PÉREZ CRUZ WELCOMES AND RECEIVES TOURISTS MONDAY TO FRIDAY. IN ENGLISH AND FRENCH, THERE ARE TWO TOURS TO CHOOSE FROM, ACCORDING TO THE AMOUNT OF WINES TASTED
DESIGN STYLE	ARCHING WOODEN RIBS SIT IN AESTHETIC HARMONY WITH THE FLUID VINA PÉREZ CRUZ TERROIR
RECOMMENDED WINES & ICEWINES	CABERNET SAUVIGNON RESERVA 2002; COT RESERVA LIMITED EDITION 2002; MERLOT; PETIT VERDOT AND SYRAH
PREMIUM VINTAGES / NEW RELEASES	2005 VINTAGE EXPECTED BETWEEN LATE MARCH AND EARLY APRIL. OTHERS INCLUDE: CARMENÈRE RESERVA LIMITED EDITION 2002 (94% CARMENÈRE COMPLETED WITH CABERNET SAUVIGNON); SYRAH RESERVA LIMITED EDITION 2002 (90% SYRAH COMPLETED WITH CABERNET SAUVIGNON); LIGUAI 2002 (35% CABERNET SAUVIGNON, 30% CARMENÈRE AND 35% SYRAH)
TASTINGS / SPECIAL EVENTS	BANQUETING FACILITIES FOR WEDDINGS, SEMINARS, WORKSHOPS, CONFERENCES AND PRODUCT LAUNCHINGS
VINTNERS	ANDRÉS PÉREZ CRUZ, PRESIDENT; GERMÁN LYON LARRAÍN, ENOLOGIST

Above: Bodegas Pérez Cruz.
Perhaps the most dramatic experience occurs in the trapezoidal void spaces left over between the vaults, as a mezzanine walkway snakes their length and pierces across the opening of the covered patio below. It's a powerful experience, and you can't help but feel as if you are secretly making your way through the building's inner sanctum

Above: Bodegas Pérez Cruz.
A void space between the flat roof and the vaults was created to facilitate natural air circulation, and this also allows for deep clerestory cuts so that spears of light can wash down the perfectly smooth wooden vaults

and tasting by the winemakers. Stretching along the flat site, the vaults kink at the building's mid section where a gaping hole becomes a covered outdoor patio for guests. The most dramatic experience, though, occurs in the trapezoidal void spaces left over between the vaults, as a mezzanine walkway snakes their length and pierces across the opening of the covered patio below. What makes this such a powerful event is that Cruz gives us the opportunity to fully appreciate and understand these pure forms from two sides. From the ground, we get to move inside the building's belly and see the arched walls rise up from their stone plinth to create a fantastic double-height room, whereas the mezzanine lets us appreciate them from the other side, feeling the power of their form as we run our hands along the outside of their curved wooden walls and caress their shape. It's a powerful experience, and you can't help but feel as if you are secretly making your way through the building's inner sanctum.

Inside, Cruz is a master in the use of light, and the winery provides visitors with a near-religious experience. A void space between the flat roof and the vaults allows for natural air circulation, and also creates deep clerestory cuts so that spears of light can wash down the perfectly smooth curved vaults.

On the outside the effect is no less fantastic, as the sinuous wooden vines and deep eaves cast seductive shadows on the curved walls of the vaults while the wood glows a warm red in the setting sun. Equally moving is the underground cellar for secondary-fermentation equipment. Here, the void-space motif is continued, as the concrete piers and heavy roof break free from their walls effectively creating a space within a space. Again, Cruz doesn't miss the opportunity to celebrate the dramatic – the roof appears to float, awash with dim light from above and from recessed lights in the polished concrete floor.

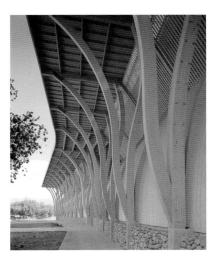

Above: **Bodegas Pérez Cruz.**
The simple wooden shed springs from the soil through a sinuous network of arched ribs that organically express the activities within, while at the same time referring to Chile's rural periphery

Opus One

Johnson Fain

Location: Oakville, California, USA
Completion date: 1991

No winery has garnered more attention in California's Napa Valley than Opus One. It's actually not that surprising since Opus is the progeny of an international partnership between Europe's celebrated Baron Philippe Rothschild of Château Mouton Rothschild and renowned Californian vintner Robert Mondavi. The partnership began to take shape in the early 1980s and resulted in an ultra-expensive and highly exclusive winery that still outshines even the trendiest newcomers. Quickly acquiring cult status among vinophiles, Opus One is unarguably the icon for high-end Cabernet and is definitely one of the valley's must-see wineries.

On naming their first-born, the story – as it is told – has the partners agreeing to choose a name of Latin origin, for easy recognition in both languages. Panning through a plethora of options from Lafayette to Alliance (the latter abandoned because Renault was planning to launch a car of the same name), the baron landed on *opus*, a musical term referring to the first work of a composer. Unfortunately, Mondavi wasn't convinced. Two hours later, and another phone call from the baron, and Opus One was born.

Set deep within 100 acres of prime Napa vines in the Rutherford Bench, the formal tree-lined approach is directly in line with the main entry. But the building doesn't rush to reveal itself, as the low-profile structure is concealed from view by a crescent-shaped berm planted with wild grasses, native wild flowers and shrubs. The softly contoured mound blends in with the backdrop of the hills and surrounding vineyards as it changes colour with the passing of the seasons. A pair of dramatic stone stairs leads up the gentle slope to gradually disclose the winery's distinctive beauty and converge at a set of framed porticoes at the edge of the semicircular entry courtyard. Shaded by olive trees, the courtyard is typically classical in its expression and ringed by arched colonnades of rusticated limestone and weathered clear redwood that connect the public areas including the front entry, reception and tasting rooms. The grounds are also impeccable – not a thing out of place. And there are certainly no wooden picnic tables anywhere, so don't expect a brown-bag lunch on the front lawn.

Visitors, especially those with an architectural bent, will appreciate the grand tour, which includes the historic Romanesque winery and its lavish grounds juxtaposed with the ultra-modern production and ageing facilities, and the vast semicircular cellar, modelled after the one at the Château Mouton Rothschild winery in France.

Designed by architect Scott Johnson (who also designed Mondavi's other

Above: **Opus One.**
Shaded by olive trees, the semicircular courtyard is typically classical in its expression and ringed by arched colonnades of rusticated limestone and weathered clear redwood that connect the public areas including the front entry, reception and tasting rooms

Opposite: **Opus One.**
The space beneath the berm shelters the Grand Chai where 1,000 first-year barrels are on display. Overlooked by the main tasting room, the vast semicircular cellar is modelled after the one at the Château Mouton Rothschild winery in France

WINERY	OPUS ONE
ADDRESS	7900 ST HELENA HIGHWAY, PO BOX 6, OAKVILLE, CALIFORNIA 94562, USA
TELEPHONE	+1 707 944 9442
WEBSITE	WWW.OPUSONEWINERY.COM
OPENING HOURS	OPEN DAILY 10AM–4PM; MAJOR HOLIDAYS EXCEPTED
TOURS	FREE TOURS DAILY AT 10:30AM; BY APPOINTMENT ONLY. OPTIONAL TASTINGS RANGE IN PRICE FROM $20 TO $65
DESIGN STYLE	CLASSICAL EUROPEAN MIXED WITH CONTEMPORARY CALIFORNIAN, THE HEMISPHERICAL FORM IS INTROVERTED LIKE A JEWELLERY BOX
RECOMMENDED WINES & ICEWINES	THE ICON FOR HIGH-END CABERNET. 1995 OPUS ONE – RUBY-GARNET COLOUR WITH A DARK BRICKISH EDGE; BLACKBERRY FRUIT, CEDAR, EUCALYPTUS, SPICE, CIGAR BOX AND MEAT AROMAS
PREMIUM VINTAGES / NEW RELEASES	OPUS ONE 1979 (SOLD AT AUCTION FOR $250); OPUS ONE 2000 (TOO YOUNG TO DRINK NOW, BUT THIS WINE WILL GROW OLD GRACEFULLY)
TASTINGS / SPECIAL EVENTS	OPUS ONE PARTNERS ROOM, TASTING ROOMS AND CELLAR DOOR OPEN DAILY 10AM–4PM
VINTNERS	BARONESS PHILIPPINE DE ROTHSCHILD AND ROBERT MONDAVI, OWNERS; MICHAEL SILACCI, VINTNER
SPECIAL FEATURES	A LITTLE-KNOWN SECOND LABEL CALLED OVERTURE THAT COSTS ONLY $40

Above: **Opus One.**
In the exclusive tony world of Cabernet Sauvignon there is no bigger player than Napa's Opus One. Set deep within 100 acres of prime Napa vines in the Rutherford Bench, the building doesn't rush to reveal itself. Concealed from view by a crescent-shaped berm planted with wild grasses, native wild flowers and shrubs, the softly contoured mound changes colour with the passing of the seasons

Right and opposite top: **Opus One.**
Clad in a rusticated white limestone, a pair of dramatic stone stairs leads up the gradual slope to meet at a set of framed porticoes at the edge of the semicircular entry courtyard

experimental vineyard, Byron in the Santa Maria Valley), the interior is flawless in its clean lines and rich polished surfaces. Hand-plastered walls are finished with a gesso of pale yet luminous yellow. The salon, which includes classic paintings ranging from Chagall to Picasso, oozes a formal ambience as 18th-century Italian opera chairs face contemporary chenille sofas and suede loungers. Nearby, brightly glazed ceramics line a 15th-century mantle.

It's easy to be impressed by the artistic touches as everything about Opus One speaks of elegance and sophistication. All the interior details including furniture, area rugs and wall sconces were specially designed to extend the architectural qualities of the building into the interior and reflect the unity of winemaking, food and art. On axis with the main entry is the Grand Stair, an opulent hulk of rich marble and polished limestone that spirals downwards beneath a beautiful elliptical clerestory, lit at night by moonlight and soft recessed downlighting.

To descend is to enter into the subterranean world of the cellars, but even these are meticulously finished with rich redwood ceilings and patterned stone walls. At the foot of the Grand Stair, the faint scent of oak wafts through. The space below the berm is devoted entirely to winemaking and includes the Grand Chai, where 1,000 first-year barrels of new French oak are on display. Overlooked by the main tasting room, the rows trace a semicircular path and appear to recede into infinity, while classic metal sconces focus parabolas of light against the stark walls. While the facility employs just 27 people and produces only one wine, the production side is an effort in pampering and perfection. Harvesters pick the grapes by hand and deliver them to the winery in small wooden boxes, each holding up to 35 pounds of fruit.

In the exclusive tony world of Cabernet Sauvignon there is no bigger player than Napa's Opus One. At $125 a bottle, it's quite possibly the most unforgettable red you'll ever have. Even if you can't take a bottle home with you, the winery is certainly the kind of place to enjoy a posh afternoon with your significant other, so take your glass and head straight to the redwood roof-top deck to enjoy the breathtaking sunset views; but don't forget, in a winery with a passion for perfection, it will always be about the wine.

Left: Opus One.
A landscaped approach to the front of the winery bisects the berm and leads to a grassed courtyard shaded by olive trees. The plan is beautifully symmetrical with the barrel-storage cellars encircling a central courtyard. Surrounding the courtyard, a covered arcade provides access to the public areas of the winery while the production areas are to the rear

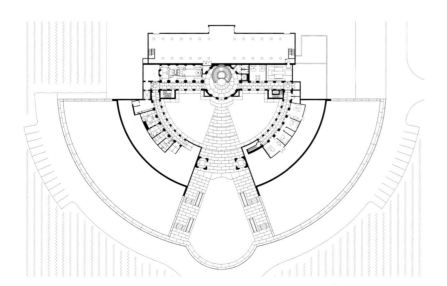

WINERY	ROSHAMBO
ADDRESS	3000 WESTSIDE ROAD, HEALDSBURG, CALIFORNIA 95448, USA
TELEPHONE	+1 707 431 2051 / 1 888 525 WINE
WEBSITE	WWW.ROSHAMBOWINERY.COM
OPENING HOURS	OPEN DAILY 10:30AM–4:30PM
RESTAURANT / CAFÉ	TASTING ROOM AND RETAIL SALES AVAILABLE
TOURS	OPEN DAILY 10:30AM–4:30PM
DESIGN STYLE	MODERN, LOW-SLUNG BUILDINGS OF STEEL, CONCRETE AND GLASS
RECOMMENDED WINES & ICEWINES	2001 SAUVIGNON BLANC, FRANK JOHNSON VINEYARDS – CRISP AND LIGHT WITH ABUNDANT AROMAS OF CITRUS (ESPECIALLY GRAPE-FRUIT), RIPE MELON AND JUST A HINT OF LEMON GRASS
PREMIUM VINTAGES / NEW RELEASES	2001 DRY CREEK VALLEY ZINFANDEL – OWNER-DESCRIBED AS: 'THINK OF THIS AS OUR BRER RABBIT MAKES A ZIN-BABY WINE. LOADED WITH RED BERRIES, SWEET, RICH TANNINS AND ALL THE PLEASURE OF HAVING JUST TRICKED THAT SLY OLD BRER FOX INTO HAVING THROWN YOU IN AMONGST ALL THAT SWEET, RIPE FRUIT.'
TASTINGS / SPECIAL EVENTS	FOR THREE YEARS RUNNING, ROSHAMBO HAS PLAYED HOST TO THE SOUTHWEST PRO-AM ROCK-PAPER-SCISSORS CHAMPIONSHIP. GALLERY WITH ROTATING ARTWORK IS ADJACENT TO THE TASTING ROOM
VINTNERS	NAOMI BRILLIANT, OWNER; JEFF IVY, VINTNER

Above left and right: Roshambo.
With a capacity of 30,000 cases, Roshambo utilises a gravity-flow winemaking system to produce Syrah, Zinfandel, Sauvignon Blanc and Chardonnay varieties. All Roshambo wines are bottled on site

Middle: Roshambo.
Roshambo offers three lines of wine: the Rock Paper Scissors; the Core; and the RPS. Cheeky names like The Obvious Sauvignon Blanc and bold graphics appeal to the palate of chic vinophiles

Right: Roshambo.
The winery's low-slung buildings are carefully integrated into the rural setting. Vaulted metal roofs impose little on the magnificent views of the mountains beyond

panorama. Bare, polished concrete floors and sparse furnishings do little to impede your view of the grapes on the vines. A wide undulating wooden ceiling seems to be the only element of excess in the otherwise naked space. With no visible columns to support it as it slopes towards the vines, a certain uneasiness overtakes you. But that is exactly the point. This is a space to experience wine and art; to question, challenge and explore. The gallery, curated by Naomi, features emerging artists with displays that change every two months. It is art with a political bent, focusing on human nature and social commentary. Not surprisingly, the gallery charges no commission with all proceeds of sales going directly to the artists.

And like the pieces of art in the gallery, the tasting bar is itself an art object, a 25-foot-long curved slab of stainless steel and white rubber. Laser-cut acrylic fins support the bar while soft white luminaires suspended from long metal wires overhead give it an ephemeral, delicate glow. The room is inviting and open, and plays the perfect host to a myriad of events. From Drag Queen breakfasts and the Super Hero/Super Villain Prom to the annual Rock-Paper-Scissors Pro-Am Invitational, these are not typical soirees for the wine and cheese set. The space can be tailored to events big or small through the use of fabric screens and recessed furniture, while a full cook's kitchen and on-site chef can cater to any culinary needs. In fact, the whole winery appears to be at the visitor's disposal. Visitors are also encouraged to explore the tank room where 29 stainless-steel wine tanks, each inscribed with the name of a personal hero from whom Naomi draws inspiration, stand at attention. A number of 'tank celebrity' events have been held to honour these individuals – the Willie Wonka party featured Roshambo's 2002 Syrah rosé paired with chocolates and candies and a screening of the film. One can only wonder what the Malcolm X party will offer.

But for all its fun and frivolity Roshambo is a serious wine producer. With a capacity of 30,000 cases and current production of approximately 18,000, it is small but its facilities are state of the art. The winery uses a gravity-flow winemaking system complemented by a bottling line. Roshambo offers three levels of wine: the Rock Paper Scissors; the Core; and the superior RPS. 'Try a bottle of The Obvious Sauvignon Blanc', says Naomi, and you too may be surprised by its distinctive character and Brilliance.

Above: **Roshambo.**
Walnut, aluminium and red-rubber seating recess into the walls of the merchandising space, creating a lounge-like ambience. Roshambo T-shirts and aprons sell alongside bottles of their award-winning Zinfandel

Above: **Roshambo.**
At the entrance, the Roshambo moniker is cut into a unique concrete water-wall. The gentle splashing of the water tempts visitors to venture further

Left: **Roshambo.**
Production facilities are split between three buildings, each progressing down with the natural grade. The gentle sweep of the curved roofs leads the eye to the view of the vineyards below

sculptures and interactive projections to illustrate the history, science, mythology and even the sensory components, that inform the making of wine.

At the entry to the vaults, what appear to be graffiti are actually ancient symbols carved into the golden-yellow plasterwork; these form a consistent theme and will follow you throughout your journey. Once inside, you essentially become a grape, streaming along the 1-kilometre path through a series of chambers that use light and sound to gently crush, ferment and press you into wine. In the fermentation vaults, the experience approaches the erotic as each of the five senses is stimulated simultaneously. Regressing deeper into the ancient cellars, 1920s viticulture and living conditions are made real while the gleaming stainless-steel fermentation tanks of the Steininger production area highlight the next pit stop. Paying tribute to mythical wine god Bacchus, seven interactive displays highlight the eternal cycles of winemaking: the pendulum of time, the moon, the wine myth, a prayer wheel, Bacchus's goat-like companion and, of course, wine god Bacchus himself. From within a golden-yellow corridor, the labyrinth blows open into a vault of the basilica, an ancient sanctuary illuminated by a sea of lights. Attention is then focused on the midnight-blue walls of the banquet hall where the feast of life and wine is celebrated with an intoxicating display of light from three gigantic chandeliers symbolising birth, love and death. Losing your bearings is actually part of the plan, as the subterranean trip secretly routes visitors underneath skylights to the linear reflecting pool above and then ascends back to the visitors' centre. Here, a wide range of wine from the entire region of Lower Austria is available for purchase.

While it is a safe bet that the Loisium will hold court as a Mecca for both wine enthusiasts and architecture buffs, the project is not yet complete. Plans also exist for a four-star boutique hotel to open in October 2005. Hoping to become a premier European destination, it will feature 82 guest rooms, a wine-themed restaurant for up to 140 guests, a cigar lounge and a speciality spa with no less than a whirlpool inside an old wine cask and a sunbathing terrace between the vine branches.

Above: **Loisium Visitors' Centre.**
The pool over underground portholes brings light into the lower tunnel

Above: **Loisium Visitors' Centre.**
Views into and from the wine store in the visitors' centre

Left: **Loisium Visitors' Centre.**
Paying tribute to mythical wine god Bacchus at the wine altar in the basilica

Solo Vino Wine Bar

Giner + Wucherer Architects

Location: Innsbruck, Austria
Completion date: 2000

After the success of the restaurant Solo Pasta, proprietor and well-known Innsbruck restaurateur Giovanni Giuseppe Conte opened Solo Vino 1+2 next door. Located on the main floor of the MCI, a side wing of the social sciences and economics faculties of the University of Innsbruck, this interesting trio of gastronomic establishments proves the old adage that there is virtue to be found in simplicity. The location of the building between Universitätsstrasse and the campus allows for a 'passage-like' eatery with two entries: one from the dense, traffic-filled old city, the other from the quiet atmosphere of the university with its nearby Hofgarten. The two university faculties form a semiborder between two distinct city quarters, now an integral part of the city and full of life.

The restaurant, Solo Pasta, presents an open aspect to the street and park, its front facade faced entirely in glass. The long narrow space is permeable and inviting. The centrally located oak-framed object containing the bar on one side with toilet facilities behind divides the space. This object reads as the largest of the straightforward furnishings, which are elegant through simplicity.

Solo Vino is a salesroom with approximately 500 hand-picked wines; delicate, typically Italian starters are served to casual customers, providing an ambience for enjoying wine and antipasti. The open, airy quality of the Solo Pasta restaurant converts within the same materiality into an intimate environment for focusing the attention on the wine. The three entities of restaurant, wine bar and storage are linked spatially, although Solo Vino is accessible from both the street and courtyard. Separated into two compartments by the bar, this 'guest room' of Solo Pasta shares a material palette with its sister restaurant. The bar, flooring and tables are milled from *Winviertler Kupfereich*, literally copper oak, from the 'wine quarter' of Lower Austria. This interesting wood actually shimmers distinctively with a copper colour. It has been planed, but left otherwise untreated, and thus allowed to acquire its famous patina. Lighting was designed by the firm Halotech, which produced small, artificially rusted steel enclosures with halogen fixtures that hang just above the tables, gently warming the food and drink below. Floodlights are used on the ceiling in close proximity to the high shelving units, thereby highlighting the wine bottles. The space itself is kept rather dark, with lighting reserved for chosen areas, resulting in an intimate atmosphere.

Other colour in the wine bar is added sparingly and carefully: there are black-painted MDF panels on the ceiling, aubergine chairs designed by Swiss

Opposite: Solo Vino Wine Bar.
In 2002, Solo Vino was extended with the 'Magnum-room', a wine-storage area housing 11,000 bottles, with shelving running along the walls lining the narrow space. Tables in the middle can seat 48 people, and can be booked for special occasions

Below: Solo Vino Wine Bar.
The centrally located oak framed object containing the bar on one side with toilet facilities behind divides the Solo Pasta space

NAME	SOLO VINO WINE BAR
ADDRESS	UNIVERSITÄTSSTRASSE 15D, 6020 INNSBRUCK, AUSTRIA
TELEPHONE	+43 512 58 72 06
OPENING HOURS	TUESDAY TO SATURDAY 10AM–12 MIDNIGHT
RESTAURANT / CAFÉ	SOLO PASTA
DESIGN STYLE	STRAIGHTFORWARD MATERIALS BELIE A DESIGN APPROACH THAT ALLOWS THE PURPOSE, MATERIALITY AND FORM TO SPEAK FOR THEMSELVES
VINTNERS / PROPRIETOR	GIOVANNI GIUSEPPE CONTE

Modernist Max Haefle and a mustard-hued wall that complements the overall colour scheme. The copper oak continues into the adjacent wine-storage room, primarily in the end-to-end shelving that covers the walls. Underfoot, the surface is comprised of a 'floating' wooden floor that is not fastened to its cork underlay but literally floats above it. The simple tables, straightforward shelving and the material palette belie a design approach that allows the purpose, materiality and form to speak for themselves. It is workmanship that is the real decoration in this design, one that relies on the craftsmanship to provide the architectural detail. And one that allows the flavour of the wine to predominate over visual taste.

Below: Solo Vino Wine Bar.
The restaurant Solo Pasta presents an open aspect to the street, its front facade faced entirely in glass

Above and left: Solo Vino Wine Bar.
The simple tables, straightforward shelving and the
material palette belie a design approach that allows
the purpose, materiality and form to speak for
themselves

Above: Solo Vino Wine Bar.
This 'guest room' of Solo Pasta shares a material palette with its sister restaurant

Below: Solo Vino Wine Bar.
A synergy of food and wine, appealing to a broad demographic, has been produced here through this interesting conjunction of the wine store, geared towards an established clientele, and the moderately priced pasta restaurant aimed at younger customers

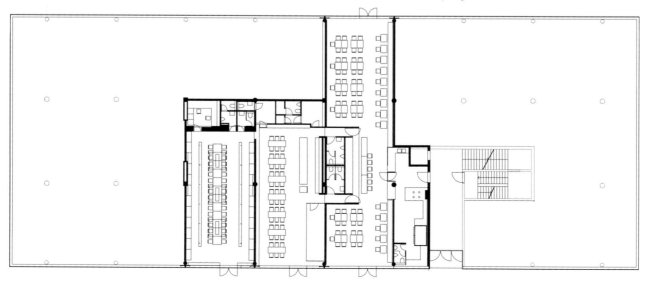

Below: **Solo Vino Wine Bar.**
The wood has been planed but left otherwise untreated,
and thus allowed to acquire its famous patina

The White Tower Restaurant

Elumin8 / Speirs and Major Associates

Location: London, United Kingdom
Completion date: 2004

The airport hotel bar conjures up images of worn-out businessmen in craggy grey suits, or stranded backpackers waiting for flights that either never arrive or never leave. Strangely devoid of anything that might make a lasting impression, they are too often full of people sitting, watching and left curious to know what sequence of travel misfortunes has conspired against their neighbour to warrant a cosmopolitan at 10 am. We seldom ask; we know we will never see them again.

The airport bar is always in transition; a place for frequent flyers to pass through on their way to somewhere else, it is rarely if ever a destination. And while mobility and transition have become the *modus operandi* for ultra-hip dot-commers and Prada-clad net-trepreneurs, in the new economy wooden chairs and artificial plants in concrete boxes simply won't do. With brand-name designers such as Philippe Starck and Karim Rashid rapidly being called upon to design *über*-lounges for the newly chic, it's no surprise then that the latest incarnation of the trendy airport lounge is the Wine Tower, a 13-metre high shimmering obelisk dedicated entirely to wine in the middle of the Radisson SAS Hotel at London's Stansted Airport.

The Radisson SAS is an ultra-chic, contemporary hotel designed specially for the business or leisure guest, and is located just a two-minute walk from the terminal gates. As what is essentially the largest and most extraordinary wine rack ever made, the Wine Tower, home to 4,000 bottles, is nothing short of a Las Vegas spectacle. The wines display their brilliance against a backdrop of coloured luminescence that ebbs and flows with its changing moods. As the tower's positively charged nucleus emits an iridescent turquoise glow, its red, white and rosé atoms circle the perimeter. Its inside is made up of a series of climate-controlled wine-storage units, each containing 12 bottles of wine. Each box is additionally illuminated with 320 individual electroluminiscent light units. To capture the attention of the sophisticated boutique-hotel guests, the tower can respond to its environment, can collectively create innumerable patterns of dancing light or even become a giant graphic equaliser for private parties. A touch-screen interface and a central computer individually control each light, rendering possible virtually any animation sequence or level of complexity. In fact, the animation variations are limited only by the staff's imagination.

The blue-green lamps are an amazing piece of science and would be impossible with conventional lighting systems. A small electrical charge is passed through a phosphorous layer causing it to glow. The technology has

Below and opposite: **The White Tower Restaurant.**
John Stuart Blackie wrote that wine is the drink of the gods. Apparently he was right. Specially trained acrobats called wine angels soar and swoop up and down within the jewelled edifice, transporting bottles of wine safely to the table

WINERY	THE WHITE TOWER RESTAURANT AND BAR (THE WINE TOWER)
ADDRESS	RADISSON SAS HOTEL LONDON STANSTED AIRPORT, WALTHAM CLOSE, LONDON STANSTED AIRPORT, ESSEX, UK
TELEPHONE	+44 (0)1279 66 10 12
WEBSITE	WWW.STANSTED.RADISSONSAS.COM
OPENING HOURS	CONTACT RESTAURANT
RESTAURANT / CAFÉ	THE WHITE TOWER RESTAURANT AND BAR
DESIGN STYLE	A 13-METRE-HIGH SHIMMERING TURQUOISE OBELISK DEDICATED ENTIRELY TO WINE
RECOMMENDED WINES & ICEWINES	VARIOUS
PREMIUM VINTAGES / NEW RELEASES	VARIOUS

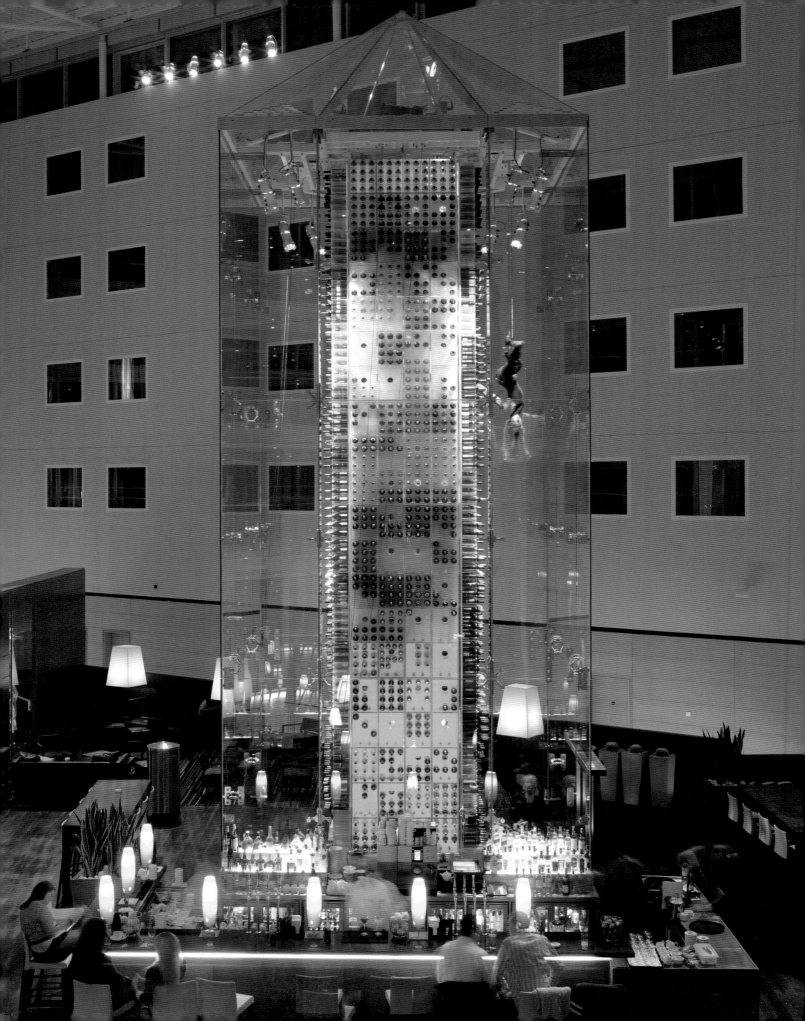

its origins in military applications, and was originally developed by NASA for their space programme. As thin as a piece of paper, the layers emit no heat, which is important in maintaining a climate-controlled environment. Bottles of white and red can be placed next to each other and be kept at the perfect temperature for drinking.

John Stuart Blackie wrote that wine is the drink of the gods; it's a fairly safe bet, though, that he never anticipated it would be plucked directly from the light and served to his table by angels. Inhabiting the fluxus zone between the charged nucleus and the glass skin, the wine angels are the real stars of the show. Specially trained acrobats, they soar and swoop up and down within the jewelled edifice transporting bottles of wine safely to the table, entertaining even the most discerning connoisseur. Having previously worked at the Millennium Dome, it's clear the angels know how to put on a show. Hoisted effortlessly by high-speed computer-controlled pulleys, they fly with the greatest of ease and provide a continually moving spectacle against the radiant backdrop of lighted panels.

The brains behind the tower are architects Jonathan Speirs and Mark Major, and lighting designers Elumin8, both UK companies. Originators of the title Lighting Architects, their proclamation is a simple one: light is all about communication. If this is indeed true, the message being delivered here is that wine is definitely the new medium of choice. The success of the Wine Tower is largely due to the burgeoning fascination with the architecture of wine, and, of course, to the fact that it is a spectacle unequalled anywhere outside Las Vegas. And while it still resides in the largely transient space of an airport hotel lounge, it might actually become a destination for travelling vinophiles.

Above: **The White Tower Restaurant.**
The inside of the tower is made up of a series of climate-controlled wine-storage units, each containing 12 bottles of wine. Each box is additionally illuminated with 320 individual electroluminiscent light units

Left: **The White Tower Restaurant.**
With brand-name designers such as Philippe Starck and Karim Rashid rapidly being called upon to design *über*-lounges for the newly chic, it's no surprise that the latest incarnation of the trendy airport lounge is the Wine Tower, a 13-metre-high shimmering obelisk dedicated entirely to wine

Opposite: **The White Tower Restaurant.**
The tower is home to 4,000 bottles, and the wines display their brilliance against a backdrop of coloured luminescence that ebbs and flows with its changing moods

Prince Wine Store

Chris Connell Interiors

Location: South Melbourne, Australia
Completion date: 2004

The traditional image of the wine store as a small, dark emporium of dusty bottles is quickly evaporating as retail outlets such as the Prince Wine Store in South Melbourne, Victoria, expand the very idea of wine retail. Following on the success of its older sibling in St Kilda, this is not so much a store for purchasing the bottled beverage as it is a hub for exploring the world of wine. Launched in late 2004, the new Prince developed from the need for a larger space, coupled with the desire for a more expansive offering of wine-related activities. These include free Saturday tastings, monthly winemaker's dinners, and courses and seminars introducing fine wines from around the world. Think interactive learning as opposed to shopping.

The clean and cool interior, designed by interior designer Chris Connell, exemplifies a contemporary approach to wine consumption and retailing. Housed in an older warehouse, the presence of the Prince on the street is practically negligible. Fronted by a nondescript dark-grey stucco blank box on a quiet street, it is entered through a glass opening punched through an otherwise vacant wall. Once inside, however, a long expanse of wood yawns under a high roof of enormous wood trusses. The open-plan design is a response to the owners' desire for uncluttered space to allow for leisurely browsing through the well-ordered displays.

The store is organised according to both wine type and price range. The owners provide a well-chosen selection of affordable wines to consumers in the entry part of the store, with the middle section devoted to varietal wines, organised first by variety, then by region. 'There is a clear journey through this store that is not only set out by the wine-type, layout and price point, but by the design highlights including the timber-lined entry tunnel and fortified wine solera', says Chris Connell.

The designer was faced with the challenge of irregular exterior walls and masonry columns lining the perimeter. The solution was to develop a camouflaging skin, inspired by the packaging of expensive wine, composed of slated timbers of raw white ash in a linear layout. Galvanised-steel wine racking and wine bins puncture this skin at extended but regular intervals. Existing materials such as the bare concrete floor were left raw, although the ductwork and roof structure were painted black with lighting placed low, so as to fade out the ceiling above. The focus is on the wine and wood, giving the impression that one is being immersed in a large barrel or in a wine crate.

This interior is all about wood in its various guises. Display-case millwork is finely detailed, with the joinery items specifically designed for each wine

Opposite: **Prince Wine Store.**
A long expanse of wood yawns under a high roof of enormous wood trusses

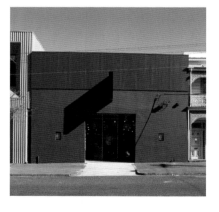

Above: **Prince Wine Store.**
Housed in an older warehouse, the presence of the Prince on the street is practically negligible

NAME	PRINCE WINE STORE
ADDRESS	177 BANK ST, SOUTH MELBOURNE, VICTORIA. 3205, AUSTRALIA
TELEPHONE	+61 3 9686 3033
WEBSITE	WWW.PRINCEWINESTORE.COM.AU
OPENING HOURS	MONDAY TO THURSDAY; 10AM–8PM; FRIDAY, SATURDAY 10AM–9PM; SUNDAY, 11AM–8PM
DESIGN STYLE	CONTEMPORARY, THE CLEAN AND COOL INTERIOR IS ALL ABOUT WOOD AND WINE
RECOMMENDED WINES & ICEWINES	VARIOUS
PREMIUM VINTAGES / NEW RELEASES	VARIOUS
TASTINGS / SPECIAL EVENTS	FREE SATURDAY TASTINGS AND MONTHLY WINEMAKERS' DINNERS
VINTNERS / PROPRIETOR	JOHN AND FRANK VAN HAANDEL, PROPRIETORS; MICHAEL MCNAMARA, PARTNER; PHILIP RICH, WINE OPERATIONS MANAGER

Above: Prince Wine Store.
Large regular intervals punctuate into the raw white ash skin with galvanised steel wine racking and wine bins

type. For example, the Riedel glassware showcase reveals the process of hand-blown lead-crystal glassware creation. The designer describes the interior as 'one enormous joinery item inserted into a void'.

Set near the rear entrance to the store, though, is the real jewel: the 'Cellar Pod'. This unique element does double duty in both replacing the small underground cellar of the St Kilda store and in providing a distinctive environment for the wine courses, tastings and seminars. In this portion of the store are wine accessories, wine books and magazines, and three solera, from which port, muscat and tokay can be bottled on demand by customers. The Cellar Pod is a freestanding wood, steel and glass box placed in the middle of the store, taking pride of place among the racks lining the walls, and visible from the entries at both front and back. Inside the pod, surrounded by the long rows of wine, is a table large enough for 20 that is used for the tastings and courses. The box is a framework of raw white ash, left unsealed to allow its natural colour to predominate. In addition to reducing costs by eliminating wood sealants, chemical use was also minimised, thereby marrying budgetary and environmental considerations. Glazed at both ends, the Cellar Pod is carefully controlled for both temperature and humidity. Learning about wine in this environment seems poetically appropriate, as visitors develop an understanding and appreciation of wine while sitting, essentially, in the cellar housing the collection.

Left and above: Prince Wine Store.
There is a well-chosen selection of affordable wines to consumers in the entry part of the store, with the middle section devoted to varietal wines, organised first by variety, then by region

Above: Prince Wine Store.
The camouflaging skin, on the right is inspired by
the packaging of expensive wine

Above: Prince Wine Store.
The joinery items specifically designed for each
wine type

Above: **Prince Wine Store.**
The Cellar Pod is for both wine storage and tastings

Left: **Prince Wine Store.**
The timber-lined rear entry tunnel

Heid Winery Tasting Room

Christine Remensberger Architect

Location: Fellbach, Germany
Completion date: 2001

The Heid Winery is a small, traditional family enterprise that has been creating wine in the German countryside since 1664. Approximately 10 kilometres from Stuttgart in southeast Germany, Fellbach is called the 'gate' to the Rems Valley (Remstal), which is also known as 'little Swabian Toscana' owing to its warm climate. The 4.5-hectare site yields about 40,000 bottles a year, produced from vines on the south side of the Kappelberg mountain. The grapes are still picked manually each year, with the help of many friends of the family, and are traditionally crushed, allowing for 14-day fermentation for the red wines. The top vintages are aged in *barriques*, and malolactic fermentation is the basis for the mild quality of the red wines. The white and sparkling wines are bottle fermented and treated with care in order to gain as much fruity aroma as possible. Interestingly, the names of all of the *barrique* and wood-aged wines are derived from the family's forefathers: the red wines are named for the men of the family, and the white for the women. For example, Melchisedec comes from Melchior; the names tend to be from the Bible and Greek mythology and are linked somehow with wine.

These details are but some indication of the family philosophy, which also translates into 'quality before quantity' and which begins with the careful tending of the vineyards, and continues into the recent design of their new tasting room and retail store. Designed by architect Christine Remensberger of Stuttgart, the tasting room/shop is a modest renovation within the ground floor of the historic, 19th-century half-timbered house in the winery grounds. The design approach was consciously in keeping with the philosophy of the winery itself and extended to materiality, lighting and furnishings.

Apart from the necessary structural interventions required to open up the space, the design minimises the elements within the space to the walls, ceiling and floor. Two rooms were created, spatially different but connected through the fluid extension of a stairway generous for such a small space. The former stable gateway forms the new entrance to the tasting room/shop. Functioning as both entry and shop window, the wood entrance door contains round inspection openings; the frameless window renders an appearance of a picture frame. The heavy load-bearing wall of the building allows for a satisfyingly deep window frame; small, but substantial.

The material palette was kept to a minimum, with light playing a key role both in articulating space and in creating cosy areas for tasting and purchasing. The detailing of the wood millwork is so minimal as to be virtually undetectable: all metal fittings and hardware are hidden. The entry area

Opposite: **Heid Winery Tasting Room.**
The shelving is placed so as to lead the visitor from the entrance up the steps to the tasting room behind

Below: **Heid Winery Tasting Room.**
The entry into the ground floor of the historic, 19th-century half-timbered house within the winery grounds

WINERY	HEID WINERY TASTING ROOM
ADDRESS	CANNSTATTERSTRASSE. 13/2, D-70734 FELLBACH, GERMANY
TELEPHONE	+49 711 58 41 12
WEBSITE	WWW.WEINGUT-HEID.DE
OPENING HOURS	MONDAY TO THURSDAY 5PM–7PM; FRIDAY 9AM–7PM; SATURDAY 9AM–1PM
DESIGN STYLE	FINELY DETAILED, MINIMALIST DESIGN INSERTED WITHIN A 19TH-CENTURY, HALF-TIMBERED HOUSE ON THE WINERY ESTATE
SPECIALTY	RED VARIETIES: TROLLINGER, LEMBERGER, SPATBURGUNDER, CUVÉES BARRIQUE: OTHER VARIETIES: SPARKLING WHITE, ROSÉ, GRAPE SCHNAPPS
PROPRIETORS	DANIELA AND MARKUS HEID
TASTINGS / SPECIAL EVENTS	SEE WEBSITE FOR MONTHLY EVENTS
SPECIAL FEATURES	TRADITIONAL FAMILY ESTATE THAT HAS BEEN MAKING WINE HERE SINCE THE 17TH CENTURY

Above and opposite top:
Heid Winery Tasting Room.
The entry area presents the wine shelving as
furnishings within the clean white space

Right: **Heid Winery Tasting Room.**
Terminating the movement from entry shop to
tasting room is a wall of wood panelling, finely
proportioned and detailed, and inset with recessed
niches for the exhibition of fine wines